Vegan
Beans
from Around
the
World

Vegan Beans from Around the World

Adventurous Recipes
for the Most Delicious, Nutritious
and Flavorful Bean Dishes Ever

KELSEY KINSER

Ulysses Press

Published by
Ulysses Press
P.O. Box 3440
Berkeley, CA 94703
www.ulyssespress.com

ISBN: 978-1-61243-285-4
Library of Congress Catalog Number 2013957410

Printed in Canada by Marquis Book Printing

10 9 8 7 6 5 4 3 2 1

Acquisitions editor: Keith Riegert
Managing editor: Claire Chun
Project editor: Alice Riegert
Editor: Beverly McGuire
Proofreader: Barbara Schultz
Front cover design: Rebecca Lown
Interior layout and design: what!design @ whatweb.com
Cover photograph: © Madlen/shutterstock.com
Index: Sayre Van Young

Distributed by Publishers Group West

This book is dedicated to New York City,
the most delicious place in the world.

Table of Contents

Introduction

◇◇

Every dish in this book is good food, not just good *vegan* food. This was the first deciding factor in whether or not a recipe made it into this publication. Personally, I am not a full-time vegan, though I do tend to prefer vegan foods for the way that they make me feel, both physically and morally.

Second, I wanted the book to be a nice mixture of "classics" and new-styled recipes that I've experienced during my travels around the globe. I've lived in Spain, France, Jamaica, and Greece and have traveled to many other lands. Currently, I call New York City home, and I work professionally as a pastry chef. It's true that New York is the melting pot of the world, and any exotic herb or spice would certainly be a short subway ride away for me. However, I have made sure that these recipes are accessible for those who don't live in New York, or India, or Mexico, or any of the lands from which some of these meals hail.

Because most of us are not spending our day-to-day lives traveling the world, we can instead indulge our wanderlust through cooking. Making a pot of cassoulet will whisk you away to the French Pyrenees; bean burritos will make you long for the surf crashing on the California coast; and, because most of these recipes are relatively light, after eating them you might feel like you actually would still have the energy to explore all these distant lands! Besides that, most of these recipes are rather inexpensive to make, which allows you to set aside more money if traveling is your ultimate goal. Even if it's not, saving money is always nice, and if you disagree, there are plenty of expensive heirloom beans that you can buy to be extravagant.

Writing this book has been a tremendous amount of fun for me. It has been a trip full of nostalgia, excitement, and learning. Making the *gigandes* instantly brought me back to my time spent in Greece, while making the crunchy green beans taught me a new (and now new favorite) snack food idea.

I have an entirely new appreciation for the almighty (yet still humble) legume. Inexpensive, healthy, delicious, and appreciated the whole world over, beans are a universal language. What more can you ask for?

Why Beans Are Important to the Vegan Diet

Beans are an important part of the diet of anyone, not just vegans and vegetarians. Beans can be found all over the world, in high-end specialty stores or in corner markets. They are a wonderful package of protein, vitamins, minerals, and flavor, all packed into an affordable and neat little bundle. When paired with rice, they form a "complete protein" that is very important for any person living on a vegetarian diet. The human body requires 21 amino acids, and the body itself creates 12 of those acids, but it needs to find the other 9 in food. A "complete" protein is a protein that contains all 9 of these acids. The most common forms of complete protein are meat and eggs, but other great examples of complete proteins are hemp seeds, buckwheat, and, of course, rice paired with beans. Beyond having protein, beans on their own are fat- and cholesterol-free and are full of fiber, potassium, folate, iron, manganese, and magnesium.

Dried Beans Versus Canned Beans

Most of the recipes in this book call for dried beans that have been soaked and then cooked. You can use canned beans for any of these recipes if that is your preference. Here are some guidelines when it comes to substituting the proper amount of canned cooked beans for raw dried beans and more. Recipes that call for dried beans also will have steps that are meant to cook the beans: usually the first step, and usually involving simmering for around 45 to 90 minutes. You will have to take this into account and skip these steps if using canned beans.

> 1 pound dry beans = 2 cups = average 6 cups cooked
>
> 1 cup dried beans = 2 to 3 cups cooked
>
> 1 (16-ounce) can beans = 2 cups with liquid, 1½ cups drained

Prepping Your Beans for Soaking and Cooking

It is this author's opinion that soaked dried beans are usually superior to canned beans. The main exception to this would be chickpeas (also known as garbanzos), which seem to be more consistent when canned without compromising on flavor. Soaking beans is one of the easiest culinary tasks imaginable, and all it requires is a little bit of forethought. Although you might groan at the idea of having to plan for tomorrow's dinner tonight, have faith because there are a plethora of reasons to soak your beans. There are a few different methods of soaking beans. You can use the long (also known as cold or overnight) soak, which requires the least amount of effort, the quick (or hot) soaking method, or the pressure cooker method. Each way has its pros and cons, and whichever manner of soaking you choose will still require a quick check and rinse of your beans. Dried beans aren't exactly clean. We're not trying to build up an immunity to dust and dirt; we're just trying to make tasty, healthy, animal-free cuisine, so let's sort and rinse these beans first. Spread the beans out on a cookie pan and scan through them to make sure there are no off-colored or pest-nibbled beans, small pebbles, or rocks among your dried little jewels. After sorting through the beans, place them in a small-holed colander (so as not to lose your beans) and rinse them well under cold water. They are now ready for your soaking method of choice.

Dried Bean Pros

Do you prefer your beans firmer or on the softer side? Soaking and cooking your own dried beans allow you greater control of the end product.

◊ Dried beans are less costly than canned beans.

◊ Dried beans produce less material waste (packaging).

◊ Dried beans have no added preservatives.

◊ Dried beans provide no exposure to BPA.

◊ Dried beans can be cooked in large batches and frozen to equal the day-to-day convenience of canned beans. Freeze the fully cooked beans laid out flat on a sheet tray (so that they do not clump together) and put them into bags in portions of 1½ cups to equal the size of a can of beans.

Canned Bean Pros

Convenience: These beans are ready to use right away.

Many recipes call for an amount of beans that is equal to the amount you find in one can.

Why You Should Soak Beans

Soaking reduces the time needed to cook dried beans, which saves time and energy. We've all heard that beans are a "musical fruit," and soaking helps to remove some of the oligosaccharide, which is a type of sugar that the body cannot break down. After about a week of regular legume eating, you should notice a marked decrease in the "intestinal upsets" caused by this tricky little sugar.

Another hint to help make beans less "upsetting" is to add some natural remedies. A few ingredients come up time and time again throughout this book, bay leaves and cumin, for example. These ingredients not only taste great with beans but also naturally help to fight the gas caused by them. Other ingredients that help with this are the herb summer savory (common in Bulgarian cuisine); epazote (a Mexican herb); and asafetida/hing powder (common in a lot of curry dishes).

Different Methods of Soaking Beans

Keep in mind these are all average times. Older beans will take longer to rehydrate and to cook; younger beans will be finished sooner. It is nearly impossible to know how old your beans are unless perhaps you go through a high-end bean purveyor such as the awesome Rancho Gordo.

Long (or Overnight) Soak

This is my preferred method, kind of a "set it and forget it" method.

1 Place the beans (rinsed) in a large glass or ceramic bowl, anything nonreactive. Cover them with cold water by about 4 inches. If you won't be able to check on the beans throughout the soaking time, add an additional 2 inches of water.

2 Let the beans soak for a minimum of 4 hours, or sometimes up to 12. Often, perfect timing is to soak the beans before leaving for work, and when you come home they are ready to be cooked. Another option is to soak them before going to bed.

3 Make sure to drain off the soaking water and rinse the beans well under cool running water. Rinsing twice is advisable if your stomach is sensitive.

Hot (or Quick) Soaking Method

This method is best for split peas, lentils, and black-eyed peas.

1 In a large pot of water, place your rinsed beans. Cover the beans with water at least twice as tall as the height of the beans. Bring the water to a rolling boil and continue to boil for 3 minutes uncovered.

2 Take the pan off the heat, cover, and allow to sit for at least an hour (but you can soak for up to 24 hours, although it negates the "quick" aspect of this method). Four hours is the average soaking time for most beans to be perfect. You can skip the covered waiting portion of this step, but then your beans will take a lot longer to cook.

3 Make sure to drain off the soaking water and rinse the beans well under cool running water. Rinsing twice is advisable if your stomach is sensitive.

Pressure Cooker Method

1 Put your rinsed beans in the pressure cooker and add enough water to cover them by 3 inches. Bring your pressure cooker up to pressure and maintain this for 5 minutes.

2 Turn the heat off and allow your cooker to depressurize naturally.

3 Make sure to drain off the soaking water and rinse the beans well under cool running water. Rinsing twice is advisable if your stomach is sensitive.

Can Beans Soak for Too Long?

Short answer: yes, but it would have to be for a very long time.

If you forget about some soaking beans and come back and see that some white has gathered on top, smell the beans. If the smell seems "off" or sour, your beans are fermenting and there is no going back. However, most likely the white is just starch from the beans and totally harmless. Fermentation is more likely to happen in a really hot kitchen. If you are worried you won't get to the beans in time, you can do a slow overnight soak in the refrigerator for at least two days. This will inhibit the likelihood of the beans going bad.

Types of Beans and Average Cooking Times

Beans come in all different shapes, sizes, and levels of readiness. You can buy dried beans, precooked canned beans, and fresh beans. Beans range in size from the tiny lentil to the large Greek *gigande* and they vary in color from solid earth tones to beautifully speckled like the cranberry bean. In fact, beans aren't even relegated to a single shape! You have the round chickpea, the aptly named kidney bean, and the wonderfully exotic Chinese long beans.

Fresh Beans

Fresh beans do not require any soaking and cook on the stove in about 15 to 30 minutes. They include:

◊ green beans

◊ crowder peas

◊ cranberry beans

◊ Chinese long beans

◊ any fresh beans that are still in the shell

Split Peas and Lentils

Commonly known as "dal" in Indian cuisine, lentils and split peas do not require soaking and cook in about a half an hour. They include split green peas, brown lentils, green lentils, French (puy) lentils, golden lentils, urad dal, and red lentils. You can swap green lentils for brown in most recipes. Red tend to be too soft.

Quick-Cooking Beans

Black-eyed peas and adzuki beans cook in about an hour and do not need to be soaked. Adzuki beans are the small red bean often found in Asian desserts.

Kidney Beans

These cook for about 2 hours if soaked, 4 hours if not soaked.

Important: *Kidney beans are unique in that they must be boiled for a minimum of 10 minutes because they contain kidney bean lectin, which is toxic.*

Examples of kidney beans include red kidney, white kidney/cannellini, and pink kidney.

Long-Cooking Beans

These cook for about 2 hours if soaked, 4 hours if not soaked. They include small red beans, pinto, anasazi, appaloosa (so named for its markings, which resemble the coat pattern of a horse), black turtle, navy/great Northern, fava, lima, chickpeas, soybeans, and edamame (which are really just the green version of soybeans). Soybeans and edamame have the highest amount of protein in all of the beans by a rather large margin. After that, most beans are comparable in the protein department.

Substituting Beans

In a pinch you can substitute many of the beans used in recipes if you are missing a variety. The main exceptions are desserts based on adzuki and a few other recipes. Rules to consider to make sure your recipe still works out:

◊ Keep it in the family: kidney beans of any color can often replace any other type of kidney bean, pintos can replace other members of the pinto family, and so on.

◊ Keep it color-coordinated: great Northern/navy beans, which are large and white, can often fill the place for *gigandes* (the Greek large white bean). Though your recipe won't be quite as authentic, it will still be delicious. Small red beans can replace red kidneys but will need less time to cook due to the size difference.

Soups and Salads

African Peanut Soup

Often people forget that peanuts are a legume and not, in fact, a nut. They are an excellent source of protein and lend a wonderful richness to any dish, be it a dessert or a one-pot wonder soup such as this African-inspired pepper rice stew.

Serves 8

¼ cup olive oil

2 medium onions, chopped

1 large red bell pepper, chopped

1 large green bell pepper, chopped

4 cloves garlic, minced

8 cups vegetable broth

1 (28-ounce) can crushed tomatoes with liquid

¼ teaspoon black pepper

½ teaspoon chili powder

¼ teaspoon red pepper flakes

½ cup uncooked brown rice

1 cup crunchy peanut butter

¼ cup chopped toasted peanuts

Cashew Sour Cream (page 43) or Tofu Sour Cream (page 44)

In a large stock pot, heat the oil on medium-high heat. Add the chopped onions and red and green bell peppers and cook until soft and browned on the edges, about 7 minutes. Add the garlic and cook another half a minute. Add the vegetable broth, the tomatoes and their liquid, and the spices. Turn heat down to low and let simmer for 40 minutes.

Add the rice to the pot and cover. Let this simmer for 20 minutes more. The rice should be nice and tender. Add the peanut butter and stir well until everything is combined. Top with chopped peanuts and vegan yogurt or sour cream before serving.

Tuscan White Bean Soup

This is one of those "whatever is left over in the fridge" kind of soups that seems fancy in the way that only rustic Italian cooking can. Have some leftover escarole? Throw it in there. Sun-dried tomatoes? Delicious, in they go. Garnish at will and pair it with some toasted or crusty bread, and you're all set.

Serves 6

1 pound cannellini beans, soaked overnight and drained and rinsed

2 tablespoons olive oil

2 shallots, chopped fine

1 celery stalk, cut into 4 pieces

1 carrot, cut into 4 pieces

3 cloves garlic, cut in half

4 cups vegetable broth

1 bay leaf

½ teaspoon freshly ground black pepper

olive oil

toasted sourdough or ciabatta bread (optional)

large flake salt

salt

Place the beans in your large soup pot and cover them with water by an inch. Bring to a boil, cover, reduce heat, and allow to simmer for 30 minutes. Drain and rinse the beans and set them aside.

Put the soup pot back on medium-high heat and heat up the olive oil. Sauté the shallots, celery, and carrot, stirring occasionally for 7 minutes, or until the vegetables are softened. Add the garlic and sauté while stirring for another minute.

Add the vegetable broth, 2 cups water, beans, and bay leaf and bring the soup to a gentle simmer. Keep the heat around medium low so that the soup is softly simmering for another 20 minutes. At this point the beans should have just begun to get tender. Add the pepper and salt the soup now to your preference and continue to barely simmer for approximately another 15 minutes or until the beans are soft but not falling apart.

Garnish this soup with large flake salt to taste, fresh ground pepper, drizzled olive oil, and toasted bread.

Sour Green Bean and Potato Soup

This soup is more like a chowder than a traditional stew but with a unique tang that keeps it from feeling too heavy. Soups like this one are abundant in the colder parts of the world such as Russia, Ukraine, and Hungary.

Serves 6

1 tablespoon olive oil

1 large onion, sliced thinly

4 red wax potatoes, cubed

1 parsnip, chopped

½ pound green beans (fresh or frozen), cut into 1-inch pieces

5 cups vegetable broth

2 tablespoons whole-wheat flour

½ cup Cashew Sour Cream (page 43) or Tofu Sour Cream (page 44)

1 tablespoon chopped fresh dill

¾ cup sauerkraut with juice

salt and pepper

In a large saucepan on medium-high heat, heat the olive oil and sauté the onion until softened, about 7 minutes. Add the potatoes, parsnip, and green beans and cook until the beans are beginning to get tender, approximately another 5 minutes.

Add the vegetable broth and bring the broth and beans to a boil on medium-high heat. Cover the pot and cook for about 15 minutes or until the potatoes are softened.

In the meantime, mix the flour into the sour cream. After the potatoes are tender, slowly add the sour cream and flour mix into the soup while stirring. Add the dill, sauerkraut with juice, and salt and pepper to taste. Cook just long enough to ensure everything is heated. Sprinkle fresh dill on top to garnish before serving.

African Curried Black-Eyed Pea and Coconut Soup

Curries are popular throughout the tropics and the combination of slightly sweet, toasty, and creamy coconut mixed with the spice of the hot pepper and curry is enough to make you feel like the Caribbean sun is shining outside even in the dead of winter.

Serves 4

1½ cups dried black-eyed peas, soaked overnight

2 tablespoons olive oil

1 large onion, chopped

1 yellow bell pepper, chopped

1 scotch bonnet pepper

3 cloves garlic, minced

2 cups vegetable broth

1 cup chopped canned tomatoes

1 teaspoon mild curry powder

1 sprig thyme

1 (14-ounce) can light coconut milk

salt and freshly ground black pepper

Rinse and drain the black-eyed peas. Put the peas in a medium-sized stock pot, bring to a boil, cover, and lower to a simmer on medium-low heat. Simmer for 1 hour or until the peas are soft. Drain the black-eyed peas and set aside.

Return the pot to medium-high heat and heat up the olive oil. Sauté the onion, bell pepper, scotch bonnet pepper, and garlic, stirring occasionally until the onion and peppers are softened, about 7 minutes. Add the broth, the black-eyed peas, tomatoes, curry powder, thyme, and salt and pepper to taste. Bring to a boil over high heat. Reduce the heat to low and simmer the stew covered for 20 minutes. Uncover, remove the scotch bonnet pepper and sprig of thyme, and add the coconut milk. Bring up to a final boil, stir to combine, and serve.

Black Bean Soup

This recipe is actually better the second day. If you have smoked salt, by all means add it to this recipe until the beans have a rich and smoky flavor that is to your liking.

Serves 4

1 tablespoon oil

1 large onion, chopped

4 teaspoons ground cumin

4 cloves garlic, minced

1 cup spicy, medium, or mild salsa, store bought or homemade

2 cups vegetable broth

1 (16-ounce) package dried black beans, soaked overnight and rinsed

1 green onion, crushed

juice of 1 lime

salt and pepper

cilantro to garnish, if desired

In a large soup pot, heat up the oil on medium-high heat. Add the onion and cook until soft and translucent, stirring occasionally, about 7 minutes. Add the cumin and garlic and stir while cooking another 2 minutes, until you can really smell the cumin getting nice and toasted. Add the salsa. Stir until well mixed.

Add the broth, 5 cups of water, black beans, and green onion. Bring to a boil, reduce heat, cover, and simmer for about 3 hours or until the beans are nice and tender.

Remove the green onion. After the beans are tender, using either a stick (also called immersion) blender or a blender or food processor, blend about half of the soup into a thick mush. Add the blended portion back into the rest of the beans. Stir in the lime juice and salt and pepper to taste. Garnish with cilantro.

Canadian Split Pea Soup

Liquid smoke is exactly the kind of ingredient that you hold off from buying because you think it's going to go unused in your cabinets, but have faith. This little bottle of wonder creates so many wonderful layers of flavor, and you can use it in nearly any recipe that might have originally called for ham or bacon. Throughout Canada, this is a restaurant and at-home staple.

Serves 8

2 tablespoons vegetable oil

2 carrots, peeled and sliced

1 celery stalk, chopped fine

1 yellow onion, diced

2 bay leaves

1 teaspoon dried thyme

5 cups vegetable broth

1 teaspoon liquid smoke

1 pound dried yellow split peas

salt and pepper

In a large soup pot, heat up the oil on medium heat. Cook the carrots, celery, onion, bay leaves, and thyme for about 7 minutes, or until the onions are translucent and the carrots are beginning to get soft.

Add the broth, 5 cups of water, the liquid smoke, and the split peas. Turn the heat up to medium high and bring the soup to a boil. Turn the heat to medium low, cover the pot, and reduce to a simmer for 1½ hours. Season with salt and pepper to taste and serve.

Lobio Nigvzit (Georgian Kidney Bean Stew)

Lobio nigvzit sounds like the name of a character out of Tolkien, but it is in fact a delightful herby and sour soup from the nation of Georgia. Like many stews, this dish gets better after a day or two of rest.

Serves 4

1 pound dried kidney beans, soaked overnight, then rinsed and drained

2 tablespoons vegetable oil

2 medium carrots, chopped fine

¼ cup celery, chopped fine

1 red onion, chopped fine

1 cup walnuts, ground fine

5 cloves garlic, minced

½ cup cilantro, chopped fine

¼ cup parsley, chopped fine

¼ cup dill, chopped fine

¼ cup red wine vinegar

1 tablespoon lemon juice

1 tablespoon ground coriander

1 teaspoon ground fenugreek

2 teaspoons salt

¼ teaspoon red pepper flakes

Place your soaked beans in a large soup pot and cover with fresh water by an inch. Cook on medium-high heat until it comes to a boil. Cover and reduce heat to a simmer and continue to cook for another 30 minutes.

While the beans simmer, in a large pan heat the vegetable oil on medium-high heat and sauté the carrots, celery, and onion until softened, about 7 minutes. Add these vegetables to the pot with the beans.

Add the remaining ingredients except for half of the cilantro. Stir to combine everything and cover and cook for another 30 minutes. The beans should be soft but not mushy. Serve garnished with the remaining cilantro.

Mesir Wat
(Ethiopian Red Lentil Soup)

Mesir wat is the name for Ethiopian red lentil stew. It's chock full of flavor from the spices and can be served either as a soup on its own (possibly topped with some cashew cheese crumbles or a dollop of vegan yogurt) or spooned heftily over rice and topped with julienned cilantro. Everyone loves a one-pot dish but so many of them have been a little too predictable. Break out of your comfort zone and ease into the flavor profiles of Ethiopian cuisine with this soup.

Serves 4

SOUP
1 tablespoon vegetable oil

1 large red onion, chopped

2 teaspoons fresh ginger, minced or grated

3 cloves garlic, minced

1 cup red lentils

1 large tomato, chopped, with seeds removed

2 tablespoons berbere spice or all the Ethiopian styled spice mix

pinch of salt

ETHIOPIAN STYLED SPICE MIX
3 teaspoons hot smoked paprika

½ teaspoon turmeric

½ teaspoon garam masala

2 teaspoons ground ginger

In a large and heavy pot, heat up the vegetable oil on medium heat. Add the onion and cook until the onion is soft and translucent, stirring occasionally, about 7 minutes. At this point add the ginger and the garlic and stir while cooking another minute.

While the onions are cooking, rinse the lentils well.

Add the tomato and all of its juices to the pot with the onions. Stir to mix and add in the spices and a big pinch of salt. Stir until completely combined. Add the lentils and 3 cups of water. Bring the pot to a boil, cover, and reduce to a simmer on medium-low heat for 40 minutes. Remove the cover and check how much water is in the pot. Turn heat up to high and cook for 10 minutes, stirring often. You want a texture that resembles oatmeal and is rather thick; add water if you need to thin out your soup or cook longer if it is too watery.

Dutch Split Pea Soup

Dutch split pea soup is quintessential comfort food. Known as either *ertwensoep* or the less appetizing name *snert,* this is a cold weather warmer.

Serves 4

4 cups vegetable broth

1½ cups dried green split peas

3 celery sticks chopped, leaves reserved and chopped

3 large carrots

1 large potato, cut into cubes

1 medium onion, diced

1 leek, sliced

TO TOP
8 ounces of smoked seitan or tempeh, sliced and cooked

In a large soup pot, bring the broth to a boil. Add the split peas, cover, and lower the heat to a simmer for 45 minutes, making sure to stir it every now and then so that the bottom does not burn.

Add the chopped vegetables and a little extra water if there is not enough to cover the vegetables. Cook for another 30 minutes or until the vegetables are nice and tender.

Blend the soup until smooth. Serve topped with chopped celery leaves and the smoked tempeh.

Githeri
(Kenyan Soup)

Githeri is a dish from Kenya that is composed of corn and beans and some seasonings. Frozen corn tends to work better in dishes like this that involve a higher heat. Don't worry about thawing the corn before using it in this recipe.

Serves 4 to 5

2 cups dried red or black beans, soaked overnight

3 cups frozen corn

4 potatoes, cut into small cubes

1 large onion, diced

3 tomatoes, chopped

1 tablespoon hot curry powder

salt and pepper

Drain and rinse the beans. Put the beans in a large sauce pot and cover with water by at least 1 inch and bring to a boil. Boil for 2 to 3 minutes. Reduce the heat and allow to simmer for 1 to 1½ hours or until the beans are softened but not mushy. Drain the beans.

Combine cooked beans with frozen corn and place back into the large sauce pot. Add just enough water to cover and bring to a boil. Add cubed potatoes, onion, tomatoes, and curry powder. Lower heat and simmer for 15 to 20 minutes, or until the potato is cooked through. Allow the water to cook down and make a stew, but if the water gets too low, add more. Add salt and pepper to taste and serve while hot.

Lentil Soup

Lentil soups are found all over the world. It was in small Greek diners, and eventually on small Greek Islands, where I found what I consider to be the singular perfect meal. Paired with toasted whole-wheat pita, you can't go wrong.

Serves 4

1½ cups brown lentils

2 cloves garlic, minced

1 celery stalk, chopped fine

1 medium yellow onion, chopped fine

½ cup peeled and chopped tomatoes

½ teaspoon ground coriander

2 bay leaves

2 tablespoons olive oil

¼ teaspoon black pepper

½ teaspoon kosher salt, or more as needed

In a medium pot combine all ingredients, including ½ teaspoon salt. Cover this blend with water and bring the entire mix to a boil. Lower the heat to medium low and simmer for 30 minutes or until the lentils have reached a firmness to your liking. Add more salt if desired and serve hot.

Miso Soup

Few dishes have experienced such a successful cultural crossover as miso soup. It's up there with sushi and one of the most commonly known (and loved) Japanese foods around. However, traditional miso soup isn't vegan; the base of many miso soups served in restaurants is dashi, a stock made from fermented fish skin and dried seaweed. The recipe calls for the use of two different types of miso paste: red (or dark) miso and white (or light) miso. If you don't want to splurge on two different types of miso, go with the light, because although the flavor won't be as deeply rich and full of umami, you will probably have more general uses for it than the red. I like to use the toasted nori sheets torn into strips. Nori is often toasted and sold in packages of sheets with which to make sushi, and having some on hand means you can make Japan's two most popular dishes without buying extra ingredients.

Serves 4

½ pound firm tofu

4 cups water

2 tablespoons red miso paste

1 tablespoon white miso paste

1 tablespoon shredded toasted nori

2 green onions

Set your tofu aside on a plate layered with either paper towels or an absorbent dish towel. Cover with another towel and press gently but firmly with your hand, applying even pressure all over. Set aside for about 15 minutes. The tofu will absorb more of the stock this way.

In a medium-sized saucepan, heat up water and both miso pastes on high heat. Bring this broth to a boil and then reduce the heat to medium high so that the water is simmering.

While the stock heats up, slice tofu into small squares. Add tofu and nori to the pot. Cook for 3 to 4 minutes.

At this time, slice the green onions thinly. Top the soup with the green onions and serve.

Ewa Dodo (Nigerian Black-Eyed Pea Stew)

Ewa dodo gets its name from the Nigerian word *ewa* for black-eyed peas and *dodo* for plantains. This stew should have a kick to it, but feel free to add more or less hot pepper to your liking.

Serves 4 to 6

2 cups dried black-eyed peas, soaked overnight and rinsed and drained

1 large onion, chopped fine

2 tablespoons tomato paste

1 teaspoon hot pepper flakes

1 cup vegetable broth

2 tablespoons olive oil

¼ cup oil for frying

green plantains, peeled and sliced

salt and pepper

Place the black-eyed peas and onion in a large pot and cover them with water by an inch. Bring to a boil, cover, reduce the heat to medium low, and simmer for an hour and a half, checking occasionally to make sure the water has not dried up completely. When the water is almost completely cooked off, add the tomato paste, hot pepper, salt and pepper to taste, and the vegetable broth. Continue to cook on a simmer while stirring every so often until the beans are tender, about 20 minutes more.

Meanwhile, heat the oil in a medium frying pan and fry the green plantains until crisp and lightly browned, about 3 to 4 minutes each side. Store on a paper towel when cooked. Serve as a side to the stew.

Bob Chorba
(Bulgarian Bean Soup)

This soup is one of the national dishes of Bulgaria. It goes by the name *bob chorba*, which translates to just "bean soup." In Bulgaria you will find three spices in every household: salt, paprika, and savory. There are two different types of savory, and if you can find it, use summer savory, which is stronger in flavor.

Serves 8

1 pound cannellini beans, soaked overnight, then rinsed and drained

2 carrots, chopped

1 onion, chopped

1 bell pepper, seeded and chopped

1 teaspoon savory (or thyme if unable to locate savory)

1 teaspoon mint

1 teaspoon paprika

½ teaspoon salt

5 tablespoons oil

1 tomato

In a large pot, bring 3 quarts of water to a boil. Add the cannellini beans, cover, and reduce to a simmer. Cook for 1½ hours or until beans begin to get soft. If any foam forms on the top of the pot, skim this off. After the beans are soft, add the carrots, onion, pepper, herbs, paprika, salt, and oil. Cook at a simmer, covered, for another hour.

Right before serving, peel and chop the tomato into small pieces and use to garnish the individual bowls of soup.

Three-Bean Salad

Everyone has probably had this salad in one form or another. It's a summertime staple and usually made of three different types of canned beans, sometimes with the addition of herbs, celery, and/or onions. In New York City you can find this salad on almost every block being sold by the pound in corner delis. It's almost just as easy to make this with cooked dried beans (and frozen or fresh blanched green beans) as it is with canned, and you will be rewarded for your effort. Canned measurements are included though.

Serves 6

2 cups cooked kidney beans, or 1 (15-ounce) can, drained and rinsed

2 cups cut blanched green beans (thawed frozen cut green beans also work well; canned are not recommended because they get mushy)

1 (15-ounce) can chickpeas, drained and rinsed

½ medium red onion, diced

½ cup chopped parsley

⅓ cup white sugar

⅓ cup apple cider vinegar

¼ cup olive oil

kosher salt

black pepper (freshly cracked is best)

Combine the beans, onion, and parsley in a large bowl.

In a smaller bowl, whisk together the remaining ingredients and season with salt and pepper to taste to make the dressing.

Pour the dressing over the beans, onion, and parsley. Toss to combine well.

Allow beans to marinate in the refrigerator for a few hours. Stir salad every hour or so to make sure the dressing is evenly distributed. Serve dish chilled. Keeps for about 3 to 4 days.

Valencian Minted Fava Salad

This salad is unexpectedly both filling and fresh. The crunch of the iceberg goes well with the freshness of the mint, and the hearty favas goes well with the earthy arugula. The bright vinaigrette ties the dish together; if topped with some tempeh or grilled tofu, it could be served as a main dish.

Serves 6

5 sprigs fresh mint, the leaves of one sprig picked and chopped and set aside

1 teaspoon whole-grain mustard

3 tablespoons red wine or sherry vinegar (Jimenez vinegar is preferred)

¼ cup extra virgin olive oil

pinch black pepper

3 cups shelled fresh favas, or 3 cups cooked favas

2 cups arugula

2 cups iceberg lettuce, chopped

1 scallion, sliced finely

salt

In a medium sauce pot place 4 of the sprigs of mint and 5 cups of water. Bring this to a boil and cover. Turn off the heat and allow the water and mint to steep for at least half an hour.

While the mint steeps, make your vinaigrette by combining your whole-grain mustard and vinegar in a medium bowl. Whisk in the olive oil and add the black pepper and salt to taste.

After the water is nice and minty add the fava beans and return the water to a boil and cook for 2 minutes. The beans should be firm but not hard in the center. Drain after the beans are ready.

Mix the beans into the vinaigrette and allow to marinate and chill in the refrigerator for at least 1 hour.

When ready to serve mix the arugula and lettuce into your serving bowl. Add the favas and the dressing. Toss well to combine and top with the chopped mint leaves and the sliced scallion. Serve.

Argentine White Bean Salad

Steak houses are common throughout Argentina, and although this book is a decidedly steak-free tome, this powerful white bean salad is more than welcome in any vegan (or non) cook's repertoire. This salad is strong enough in both flavor and its ability to fill you up to take the center stage of any dinner party. If you can find the Argentinian pepper *aji molido*, feel free to use it, or partially grind red pepper flakes for a similar spice.

Serves 4

1 red pepper

1 yellow pepper

2 cups dried white beans, soaked overnight and then rinsed and drained

1 teaspoon liquid smoke

1 yellow onion, quartered

2 cloves garlic, minced

2 teaspoons red pepper flakes (or *aji molido*)

⅛ teaspoon salt (kosher salt preferred)

2 tablespoons sherry vinegar

1 tablespoon Dijon mustard

1 tablespoon olive oil

4 green onions, chopped

6 cherry tomatoes, halved

store-bought or homemade seitan chorizo sausages, cooked

¼ cup parsley, chopped

Preheat the oven to 500°F.

Place the whole bell peppers on a tin foil–lined sheet tray and bake for 30 to 40 minutes, or until the skins of the peppers are thoroughly charred and very wrinkly. Flip the peppers every 10 minutes to ensure even roasting. After the peppers are ready, cover them tightly with aluminum foil and allow them to cool enough for you to be able to handle them. Remove the stems and halve the peppers. Peel off the skin and scoop out the seeds. Discard these. Julienne the roasted pepper flesh and set aside.

During the same time place the beans, liquid smoke, and onion into a medium-sized pot and cover with water by an inch. Bring to a boil on medium-high heat, cover, reduce heat, and simmer for 1½ hours. The beans should be tender but not mushy. Drain the beans but reserve 1 cup of the cooking liquid. Cook down this reserved liquid until it is thickened. Stir in the garlic, pepper flakes, salt, vinegar, Dijon, and olive oil. Remove from heat.

In a large bowl, toss together the beans, green onions, peppers, tomatoes, seitan, parsley, and seasoned cooking liquid. Serve.

Greek Lentil Salad

Lentils, also called *fakes* in Greek, are found in every home throughout the country. They don't require the soaking time that beans do, and they come in a wide variety of colors and flavors. The brown lentil is the dominant variety in Greece. French "puy" lentils offer a more delicate flavor if you want to substitute them. This is a lovely chilled summer salad.

Serves 4 as a side

2 cups lentils

2 bay leaves

1 cinnamon stick

½ cup olive oil

1 medium-sized red onion

3 oranges

sea salt and black pepper

Rinse the lentils well and make sure there are no pebbles or discolored lentils in the mix.

In a medium pot, combine the bay leaves, cinnamon stick, ¼ cup of olive oil, and the washed lentils. Cover everything with water by at least 1 inch and bring this mixture to a boil. Reduce heat and simmer for 15 to 20 minutes or until lentils are cooked through.

While lentils are cooking, slice the red onion thinly and peel and segment 2 of the oranges.

Drain the cooked lentils and allow to cool. Discard the bay leaves and cinnamon stick.

In a medium bowl, juice the remaining orange and mix this juice with the leftover olive oil, and salt and pepper to taste until well combined. Toss with the cooked lentils and refrigerate for an hour, tossing once after 30 minutes and once before serving.

Before serving, add the orange segments and sliced red onion.

Sookju Namul (Korean Mung Bean Salad)

Healthy, quick, and goes with any Korean meal, *sookju namul* is a refreshing salad of mung bean sprouts that you'll find at almost every Korean table. It is also one of the foods served during Chuseok, the Korean harvest festival.

Serves 5

3 cups water, boiling

1 teaspoon kosher salt

4 ounces fresh mung bean sprouts, rinsed

1 clove garlic, minced

1 teaspoon roasted sesame seeds

½ teaspoon ground salt, or more to taste

1 tablespoon sesame oil

1 green onion, sliced thin

Bring the water to a boil in a medium pot and add the teaspoon of kosher salt. Blanch the bean sprouts by dunking them in the boiling water for a minute. Remove them from the salted water but do not drain.

In a small bowl, mix together the garlic, sesame seeds, salt, and sesame oil.

Toss together the sprouts and green onions and sesame oil dressing. Serve completely cooled.

Malaysian Vegetable Salad

There are many different versions of salads like this (known as *pecal* in Malaysia) from this region of the world, and you are more than welcome to try tossing different things in your salad. Not a big tempeh fan? Try seitan. Avoiding tofu? This works great with sliced cooked portobello mushrooms. The sauce recipe has been adapted to be more accessible to the American kitchen.

Serves 6

PEANUT SAUCE
½ cup oil for frying, divided

1 cup roasted peanuts

1 clove garlic, minced

1 shallot, minced

1 Thai bird's eye chile, chopped

5 kaffir lime leaves (found in Asian grocers) *or* juice and zest of 1 lime

2 tablespoons brown sugar

1 tablespoon salt

1 tablespoon grated ginger or galangal

1 tablespoon crumbled toasted nori (optional)

SALAD
½ cup extra firm tofu, pressed and cubed

½ cup tempeh, cubed

½ small red onion, sliced thinly

½ cup green beans, cut into 1- to 2-inch pieces

½ cup fresh mung bean sprouts

1 small cucumber, halved and sliced thinly

In a large frying pan, heat ¼ cup of oil on medium-high heat. Fry the peanuts until deeply golden brown; let peanuts rest on paper towels to absorb some of the oil. After peanuts are cooled, grind in a food processor until the peanuts are fine pieces.

Add the garlic, shallot, and chile to the pan and fry for about 3 minutes on medium-high heat. Add the lime leaves or zest and juice, brown sugar, salt, ginger, and nori to the food processor and chop until a paste is formed. Add the peanuts and process just until combined. Set aside.

Heat up the remaining oil in the frying pan on medium-high heat and fry the cubed tofu and tempeh until golden brown, stirring occasionally, about 7 minutes. Mix the tofu and tempeh in a large bowl with the onion, green beans, bean sprouts, and cucumber.

Mix 1 cup of warm water into the peanut-based paste until the paste is liquid. Cover the mixed vegetables with peanut sauce and toss well to combine.

Southwestern Style Salad

This is the kind of salad that can easily be made into a meal. Toss it on a bed of rice or lettuce or roll it up into a tortilla, and you have a deliciously flavorful lunch or dinner. Feel free to top this off with heaps of guacamole or vegan sour cream.

Serves 4

⅓ cup olive oil

1 lime, juiced

½ teaspoon salt

1 teaspoon chili powder

½ teaspoon ground cumin

3 cups cooked pinto beans, approximately 1 cup dried or 2 (15-ounce) cans

1½ cups corn

1 green bell pepper, diced

½ red onion, diced

3 tomatoes, chopped

4 green onions, chopped

¼ cup fresh cilantro, chopped

In a large bowl, stir together the olive oil, lime juice, salt, chili powder, and ground cumin.

Add the remaining ingredients and toss together to combine. Serve chilled or at room temperature.

Indonesian Raw Veggie Salad

Like many recipes, this salad has evolved over time, but it's the distinctive peanut sauce that makes it so popular and iconic. This variation of raw vegetable salad comes from Indonesia and goes by the name *karedok*.

Serves 4

SAUCE

2 red chiles

1 clove garlic

5 small red chilies

½ teaspoon *kencur* (optional)

2 cups peanuts, roasted and ground

1 tablespoon palm sugar (or brown sugar)

2 tablespoons vinegar

1 teaspoon tamarind paste

1 teaspoon salt

⅔ cup hot water

SALAD

4 ounces bean sprouts

4 ounces cucumber, sliced

3 cabbage leaves, chopped fine

large handful (about 1 ounce) basil leaves, cut into strips

4 ounces green beans, cut into 1-inch pieces

Using either a food processor or blender, combine the red chiles, garlic, *kencur*, peanuts, palm sugar, vinegar, tamarind paste, salt, and water until smooth.

In a large bowl, toss together the bean sprouts, cucumber, cabbage leaves, basil, and string beans. Top with the sauce and serve.

Southeast Asian Vegetable Salad

Vegetable salads composed of beans are very common throughout Southeast Asia. This style of salad goes by the name *acar*.

Serves 4 as a side

SPICE PASTE
5 shallots

12 fresh red chiles

½ teaspoon ground turmeric

2 macadamia nuts

½ teaspoon tamarind paste

SALAD
5 tablespoons vegetable oil

¾ teaspoon salt, or more if needed

¾ teaspoon sugar

⅔ pound cucumber, cut lengthwise with seeds and skins

⅓ pound cabbage, torn into large pieces

2 ounces carrot, cut lengthwise

2 ounces green beans, cut into 1-inch pieces

2 ounces Chinese long beans, cut into 1-inch pieces

⅓ cup peanuts, roasted and ground

In a food processor combine the shallots, red chiles, turmeric, macadamia nuts, and tamarind paste. Blend until this becomes a thick paste.

Using either a wok or large pan, heat up the oil on medium-high heat. Add the spice paste while stirring. Stir fry for about 3 minutes. Add 1 cup water. Allow this mix to boil. Add the salt and sugar. This mixture should be very hot and bubbling.

Add all the vegetables, stir once to combine, and remove from heat. Top with the ground peanuts.

Allow to cool and serve.

Sides and Snacks

Cashew Sour Cream

While technically this recipe is bean-free it is just too good not to include and can be used to compliment any of your bean-based dishes wherever sour cream is called for. If you prefer to avoid soy or are simply looking for a less processed option than store-bought tofu-based sour cream, this is the recipe for you. Not counting the overnight soaking, this is one quick and satisfying side to make for yourself. Make sure that you are using raw cashews, not the salted or roasted ones. Don't skimp on the soaking, or your sour cream will have a mealy and unappetizing texture. Use the following recipe as a guideline, but if you want more tang, adjust the vinegar to your tastes. Because this will last for a week if kept covered in the refrigerator, you can make it ahead of time.

Serves 8

1 cup raw cashews, soaked overnight and rinsed and drained

¼ cup cold water

1 lemon, juiced

1 teaspoon apple cider vinegar

¼ teaspoon salt

In a food processor or high-powered blender, combine all ingredients until completely smooth.

Allow to rest in the refrigerator for at least two hours or until completely chilled. Use wherever sour cream is called for.

Tofu Sour Cream

This is a quick and delicious substitute for dairy sour cream. Use it anywhere a recipe calls for sour cream, cup for cup. It's an excellent way to garnish a lot of the soups and stews in this book.

Serves 8

1 (16-ounce) package silken tofu

1 teaspoon olive oil

2 tablespoons lemon juice

2 teaspoons apple cider vinegar

1 teaspoon sugar

1 teaspoon salt

Combine all ingredients in a blender and mix until completely smooth, for at least 3 minutes. Strain through a fine mesh strainer if your blender is not very powerful.

Refrigerate for a minimum of an hour to allow it to cool completely and to thicken up slightly.

Mujadara
(Lebanese Spiced Lentil Pilaf)

Don't let the simplicity of this dish fool you. It provides an immense complexity of flavor and an intensely heady and exotic aroma that will fill your kitchen while you caramelize your onions and cook your spiced lentils. The slightly sweet and spicy fragrance of the cinnamon blends perfectly with the distinctly savory garlic. This dish is delightfully rich without being heavy. I got the recipe for it years ago from a Lebanese man who worked in one of New York City's most well-known spice shops, Kalustyan's, where this dish is served as a side or stuffed into a pita to make a sandwich deserving of its cult following. The combination of lentils and bulgur creates a complete protein, giving you all of your essential amino acids without the cholesterol found in animal proteins.

Serves 4 to 6

4 tablespoons olive oil

3 medium onions, sliced thin

2 to 2½ cups vegetable broth (or water)

3 cups brown or green lentils (not French or red)

1 cinnamon stick

½ teaspoon ground allspice

1 bay leaf

1 cup bulgur (or brown rice)

salt and pepper

First you will need caramelized onions. These can be made days in advance, and I always have some on hand. It takes some practice to find what constitutes the "perfect" caramelized onions to suit your own tastes. For me, the closer to burned (without crossing that threshold), the better. I go for a quick caramelization over high heat and deglaze my pan often (deglazing is the act of splashing liquid onto a hot pan to loosen all those tasty little burned bits off of the bottom of the pan), which essentially coats the onions in a gravy of their own deliciousness.

Until you find your own preferred level of caramelization, though, you should work more slowly. Add 4 tablespoons of olive oil to a large pan over medium-high heat. Let the oil heat up and add your thinly sliced onions. They should sizzle and serenade you. You want to stir these onions just enough that they do not burn. If you stir too often, they won't have a chance to develop any color. That's what you are looking for: a nice yellow that eventually turns into a deep chestnut brown. (Never black, because black onions are burned onions, and they give off a bitterness that nothing can cover.) The smell should be definitely savory with a hint of sweet. If you're having a problem with the onions sticking to the bottom of your pan, add ¼ cup or so of vegetable broth and stir quickly, scraping the bottom of the pan. Then turn your heat down to medium. The onions will cook down in size quite a bit. Make sure to taste-test as you go, and when you reach a point where your onions are soft, and brown, and taste somewhat sweet, you've got the perfect caramelized onions. This should take on average 20 to 30 minutes.

If you make your onions beforehand, you will need to heat half of them back up when starting to make the rest of the dish. Do this in the same large saucepan in which you caramelized them.

Gather your lentils into a medium saucepan and cover with cold water by a couple of inches. On medium-high heat, bring your water and lentils to a boil. Lower your heat until the lentils are just simmering. Allow them to simmer for about 10 minutes. You want them about half cooked. Drain them.

If you have not yet caramelized your onions, now is the time to do so. You can start the onions to cook while you are simmering your lentils. After your onions are fragrant and transformed from their former self, take about half of them out of the pan and keep them to garnish the top of the *mujadara*. Add the cinnamon stick, ground allspice, bay leaf, partially cooked lentils, bulgur (or rice), 2 cups of vegetable broth, and salt and pepper to taste. Turn the heat up to medium-high until this begins to boil. Now cover the pan, reduce your heat to low, and simmer for 30 minutes. Your liquid should at this point be fully absorbed by the bulgur and lentils. If you still have too much broth, let it cook an additional 5 minutes. If you run out of broth early, add another ½ cup during the cooking. After you think it is done (when the bulgur is soft and the liquid is gone), turn off the heat and let the dish rest, covered, for 5 minutes.

To serve, top with the reserved onions and eat as is or stuffed into a pocket of pita bread.

Mexican Refried Beans

A classic recipe that goes great in burritos or chili alike.

Serves 4 to 6

2 cups dried pinto beans

7 cups cold water

1 cup chopped tomatoes, fresh or canned

2 sprigs dried epazote or ¼ teaspoon crumbled epazote (optional)

½ large onion, chopped

1 teaspoon kosher salt

¼ cup vegetable shortening

1 teaspoon garlic, minced

1 serrano chile, cut in half and seeds removed

¼ teaspoon black pepper

In a large pot combine beans, water, ½ cup of the tomato, epazote, and half of the chopped onion. Bring this mixture to a boil, lower the heat to a simmer, and let cook for 1½ hours, partially covered.

After 90 minutes have passed, taste test one of the beans. If it is soft but not yet mushy, add the salt and continue to simmer over very low heat for another half an hour. The beans should begin to get mushy, and the water should be nearly gone. As the water level gets low, you will want to stir the pot occasionally to prevent the beans on the bottom of the pan from burning.

During the last 15 minutes or so, heat 2 tablespoons of the shortening in a large frying pan. The shortening should be a clear liquid and giving off quite a bit of heat when it is ready. Fry the last half of chopped onion and lower the heat to medium. Cook for about 7 minutes. The onion should be soft and more translucent but not browning. Add the garlic and chile. Cook for half a minute longer. Add the remaining tomatoes and black pepper and cook at a simmer for 3 minutes.

Drain the beans and have them ready to add to the frying pan. After the tomatoes have been simmering, add ¼ cup of the beans to the pan and mash them with either the back of a fork or a spatula. Keep adding the beans and mashing, ¼ cup at a time. If the mixture begins to get too dry, add some more shortening 1 tablespoon at a time. After all of the beans have been added and mashed, cook for 10 minutes over low heat, making sure to stir very frequently until the beans are dry and thick. Enjoy.

Boston Baked Beans

It seems sweet and tangy baked beans are a specialty of many regions, but this Boston style is the one with which most Americans are familiar. After trying these, you can't go back to canned.

Serves 6

2 cups navy beans, soaked overnight and drained and rinsed

3 tablespoons blackstrap molasses

2 teaspoons salt

¼ teaspoon freshly ground black pepper

½ teaspoon dry mustard

½ cup ketchup

¼ cup brown sugar

2 teaspoons soy sauce

1 teaspoon apple cider vinegar

1 teaspoon liquid smoke

1 onion, chopped finely

Cover the beans with water by an inch in a medium-sized pot and cook on medium-high heat until boiling. Reduce heat to medium low and allow to simmer until beans are tender, about 1½ hours. Drain the beans.

Preheat the oven to 325°F.

In a small pot, stir together the molasses, salt, pepper, mustard, ketchup, brown sugar, soy sauce, vinegar, and liquid smoke and bring this sauce to a boil.

Place the beans and onion in a small oven-safe dish. Pour the sauce over the beans and add fresh water to barely cover the beans.

Bake for 3½ hours, covered, until the beans are soft and flavorful. Check throughout cooking to see if the beans need any water; you want a thick sauce surrounding the beans. If they are getting too dry, add a couple splashes of water.

British Baked Beans

It might seem odd to Americans, but many Brits consider these beans to be a distinct part of a traditional British breakfast (which is most certainly not vegan). However, these beans are delicious, especially served on some toast with a little peeled Roma tomato alongside and some tofu scramble.

Serves 6

2 tablespoons vegetable oil

1 large sweet yellow onion, diced

2 stems thyme, leaves taken off of stem

1 bay leaf

pinch ground cloves

3 cloves garlic, minced

1 stalk celery, chopped

¼ cup brown sugar

2 teaspoons salt

2 teaspoons hot sauce (Tabasco style)

2 tablespoons ketchup

5 cups peeled canned Italian tomatoes and juices, chopped

3 cups navy beans, soaked overnight

1 tablespoon sherry vinegar

In a large pot, heat the oil over medium-high heat and cook the onion until softened and browned, stirring occasionally, about 7 minutes. Add the herbs, spices, garlic, and celery. Cook while stirring another 2 minutes. Add the sugar, salt, hot sauce, ketchup, tomatoes, and sherry vinegar. Cover and simmer for 30 minutes, making sure to stir every now and then so that nothing catches on the bottom of the pan and burns. You want the sauce to look thick, red, and similar to a loose jam.

Add the beans and simmer covered for at least 45 minutes. You want the beans to be very soft, almost mushy. This dish will keep well refrigerated for about a week and tastes better the second day.

Chickpea Chips

Trying to avoid corn but still want tortilla-style chips? Want to slip a little more protein into your snacking? Try these chips then. Chickpea flour is commonly found in health food stores or in Indian markets under the name gram flour.

Serves 2 to 4

1 cup chickpea flour

½ teaspoon kosher salt

pinch fresh ground black pepper

1¼ cups water

2 tablespoons olive oil

Preheat the oven to 350°F.

Combine the chickpea flour with the salt and pepper. Whisk in the water and then the oil. Make sure to whisk well so that you have a smooth batter.

Heat a large nonstick frying pan on high heat. You can test for pan readiness by sprinkling a droplet of water onto the pan. It should pop and sizzle. After the pan is very hot, pour ⅓ of the batter into the pan. You might need more or less depending on your pan size. Ultimately you want a thin layer about the same thickness as a tortilla. After the bottom of the chickpea pancake is nice and browned (about 3 minutes), you can slide it off the pan onto a cutting board and cut it into triangles (or you can just cook the entire thing and break it into uneven pieces.) Set the pieces aside on a large baking sheet. Repeat with the rest of the batter.

Bake the chips for approximately 15 to 20 minutes or until they are browned and crispy. Serve.

Crispy Roasted Edamame

Frozen edamame is like a gift from the heavens, and you should always have some on hand. If you have edamame in the shells, simply steam them and serve them with a little sea salt on top. If you have preshelled edamame, try roasting them for a crunchy guilt-free snack.

Serves 6

1 (12-ounce) package frozen and shelled edamame, thawed
1 tablespoon olive oil
1 teaspoon garlic powder
salt and pepper

Preheat the oven to 400°F. Line a cookie tray with aluminum foil.

Place your edamame in a medium-size bowl and add the olive oil, garlic powder, and salt and pepper to taste. Toss to coat the edamame well.

Spread the edamame onto the cookie tray and bake for 15 minutes, stirring once halfway through so that they do not burn.

Crunchy Roasted Chickpeas

This is more of a snack than a side, but it's about time snacks got the respect they deserve. This recipe is deceptively simple, inexpensive, and totally customizable to your tastes. Stop spending so much on fancy vegan snack mixes and impress your friends at your next party or just spoil yourself.

Serves 4 to 6

1 tablespoon sriracha

1 tablespoon cinnamon

3 tablespoons chili powder

½ teaspoon salt

big pinch black pepper

3 tablespoons brown sugar

2 tablespoons olive oil

2 (15-ounce) cans of chickpeas, drained and rinsed

Preheat the oven to 400°F.

In a large bowl, combine all of the spices, sugar, and olive oil. Add the chickpeas and mix until the chickpeas are completely coated by the spice mixture.

Spread the chickpeas out on the baking sheet into a single even layer. Bake until crisp but not burned on the middle rack for about 40 minutes.

Feel free to experiment with your own spices. Different chili powders and curries work wonderfully in place of the sriracha, sugar, and other spices. Have fun!

Fasolakia (Greek Green Beans)

I grew up next to a Greek restaurant, and if you did not get that classic, the Greek salad, with your meal, you got this ubiquitous Hellenic side. Now I love green beans in all forms, but there is just something about this marriage of full-bodied olive oil and deeply summery tasting tomato paste being delivered by perfectly tender (but never soggy) green beans that brings me back to my childhood. The secret to this dish is the baking soda, which keeps the cell walls of the beans intact even when faced with the acidity of the tomatoes, so your beans don't turn to mush during the long cooking time.

Serves 4 to 6

5 tablespoons extra virgin olive oil

1 medium onion, chopped fine

4 garlic cloves, minced

pinch cayenne pepper (optional)

1½ cups water

½ teaspoon baking soda

1½ pounds green beans, fresh trimmed and cut into 2- to 3-inch pieces or frozen (which normally come cut already)

1 tablespoon tomato paste

1 (14.5-ounce) can diced tomatoes, drained with juice reserved, chopped coarse

1 teaspoon salt

¼ teaspoon pepper

red wine vinegar

Preheat the oven to 425°F.

In a Dutch oven or large oven-safe pot with lid, heat 3 tablespoons of extra virgin olive oil over medium-high heat. After the oil is hot, add the chopped onion and cook, stirring occasionally, until the onion is tender and slightly translucent, about 10 minutes. Toss the garlic and cayenne into the pot and stir continuously until the smell of garlic, onion, and cayenne begins to fill the air, about 30 seconds.

Pour in the water, baking soda, and green beans and bring to a bubbling simmer. Reduce heat to medium-low and cook, stirring occasionally, for 10 minutes. Stir in tomato paste, tomatoes and their juice, salt, and pepper.

Place the cover on the pot and move the dish into the oven. Cook until the sauce is slightly thickened (similar to a pasta sauce) and the green beans are soft enough that you could slice them with your fork, 40 to 50 minutes. Sprinkle with vinegar to taste.

Drizzle with remaining 2 tablespoons olive oil and serve warm or at room temperature. This dish is remarkable the second day, when all of the flavors have really had a chance to blend.

Variations

Okra: 1½ pounds fresh okra or two 10-ounce packages of frozen okra, thawed. Trim off the conical tops of the fresh okra if using fresh. Before cooking, marinate the okra in ½ cup red wine vinegar, tossing every 15 to 30 minutes for 1 to 2 hours. Rinse under cold water before adding to the garlic, onions, and cayenne. Omit the baking soda.

Cauliflower: 3-pound head of cauliflower broken into florets. Omit the baking soda but cook the same as the green beans.

Green Bean Fries

These "fries" are going to be the next kale chip; just you wait and see. These are becoming more and more popular in the up-and-coming artistic neighborhoods of Bushwick and Williamsburg in Brooklyn, New York City.

Serves 4

2 cups fresh green beans, ends cut off, or 1 pound frozen green beans, thawed

1 tablespoon olive oil

¾ teaspoon kosher salt

fresh ground black pepper to taste

2 tablespoons nutritional yeast

1 teaspoon onion powder

1 teaspoon garlic powder

Preheat the oven to 425°F. Line a sheet tray with aluminum foil or parchment paper.

In a large bowl toss your beans in the olive oil. Lay out on the sheet tray completely flat (bunched up beans will not get crispy).

Mix together the remaining ingredients. Sprinkle evenly over the beans.

Bake for 12 minutes. Carefully broil for another 1 to 2 minutes. Be sure not to broil for longer, or they will burn. Serve.

Favas with Sautéed Greens

Favas are plentiful in the Mediterranean, and there are many versions of recipes like this in that region. In the Greek Islands you might find them with lemon-accented pickled red onion and capers, but in Italy greens take the supporting role in this bright and satisfying dish. Chicory is the favored green of the southern Italians, and spinach will never fail you, but for that iconically Italian taste go for broccoli rabe (also known as baby broccoli).

Serves 6 to 8

5 tablespoons olive oil

½ large yellow onion, chopped

2 cloves garlic,

1 tomato, seeded and chopped

1 pound dried fava beans, soaked overnight, rinsed, and drained

2 pounds broccoli rabe

pinch fresh nutmeg

sea salt

fresh ground black pepper

In a medium pot, heat 2 tablespoons of the olive oil and sauté the onion, stirring occasionally until the onion is softened, about 7 minutes. Add the garlic and cook for another minute. Add the tomato and stir to coat with oil. Add the drained beans and cover everything with water by an inch. Cover and bring to a boil. Reduce heat and simmer for 2 hours or until beans are very soft, nearly mushy. Salt to taste.

In a large frying pan, heat up 2 tablespoons of olive oil. Sauté the broccoli rabe until it is completely wilted and soft, stirring from time to time. Grate just a pinch of fresh nutmeg onto the rabe. This will help to temper the bitterness. Set aside.

Using either a potato masher or a food processor, mash the fava beans with the onion, garlic, and tomato. Place into a bowl, top with the wilted rabe, and drizzle the last tablespoon of olive oil. Top with salt and pepper to taste, then serve.

Cuban Black Beans

Cuban food is everywhere to be found in south Florida, but it is surprisingly not as popular as it deserves to be outside of this part of the nation. Hopefully recipes like this one will help to change that. Black beans are a staple in Cuban food, and garlic and cumin are the perfect accents to them.

Serves 6

1 pound dried black beans, soaked overnight, then drained and rinsed

1 red bell pepper, chopped

¼ cup olive oil plus 2 tablespoons olive oil, separated

1 large onion, diced

1 green bell pepper, chopped fine

5 cloves garlic, minced

1 teaspoon sugar

2 bay leaves

1 teaspoon ground cumin

4 teaspoons salt

½ teaspoon fresh ground black pepper

¼ teaspoon dried oregano

2 tablespoons apple cider vinegar

2 tablespoons wine

Place the beans and red bell pepper in a large pot and cover with water by 1 inch. Bring the water to a boil, cover, and reduce heat to a simmer on medium low. Cook the beans until they are tender, but not mushy, approximately 30 to 45 minutes.

Heat the ¼ cup of oil on medium-high heat in a medium-sized pan. Sauté the onion, green bell pepper, and garlic and cook until soft, stirring occasionally. Measure out 1 cup of the cooked beans and add them to the onion, bell pepper, and garlic. Mash them all together with a fork. Add the mashed beans mixture to the pot of cooking black beans. Add the sugar, bay leaves, cumin, salt, black pepper, and oregano. Turn heat up to high and cook on a boil for another hour. If the beans are too wet, continue to cook on a higher heat.

Add the vinegar and wine. Keep covered and simmer on a medium-low temperature and cook for another hour. Add the last 2 tablespoons of olive oil right before serving.

Gigandes (Greek Giant White Beans)

Gigandes, or Greek giant white beans, are not only popular in the Mediterranean. We used to make these every other day at my first kitchen job. They are hearty enough to be a great winter meal when served heated and fresh enough when chilled to make a lovely summer side dish. Basically you can't go wrong when you serve these.

Serves 4

1 pound dried giant Northern white or lima beans (soaked overnight)
1 large yellow onion, finely chopped
3 tablespoons olive oil
2 garlic cloves, minced
2 large tomatoes, peeled and finely diced
2 tablespoons finely chopped dill
2 bay leaves
1 cup water
1 tablespoon tomato paste
salt and pepper

Preheat the oven to 350°F.

Reconstitute the beans that you have soaked overnight. Drain them, rinse them, drain once more, and place them in a large dutch oven or saucepan. Fill the pan with cold water until the water covers the beans by about 1 to 2 inches. Bring the water to a boil. Reduce the heat and allow the beans to simmer for around 45 minutes or until most of the water has been absorbed. Drain the beans and rinse them under cold water to cool them and stop them from cooking any further. You do not want mushy beans.

During this simmering time, sauté your onion in a large skillet with the olive oil over medium heat for about 10 minutes. Your onion should be soft and somewhat translucent. Add the garlic and sauté for

1 more minute. Add the diced tomatoes and allow this all to simmer for approximately another 10 minutes.

Return the beans to the Dutch oven if using and add the onion, garlic, and tomato mix and remaining ingredients. Season with salt and pepper to taste. If you used a sauce pot, transfer all of the ingredients to an oven-proof dish. Bake this on the middle oven rack for 1 to 1½ hours or until the beans have taken in most of the sauce. If the beans look a little burned (but not black) on top, then you have exactly what you are looking for.

Frijoles Colombianos (Colombian Red Beans)

This traditional Latin American dish is normally made with pork. In its place I recommend a combination of liquid smoke (found in the seasonings section of most grocery stores), onion powder, and smoked paprika. This hearty recipe is great mixed with rice or alone and often finds its way into burritos, queso-less-dillas, or anything else that needs to be amped up a bit. Pairs perfectly with salsa (the food and the music) and fried sweet plantains.

Serves 4 to 6

3 tablespoons olive oil

1 large tomato, roughly chopped

1 tablespoon brown sugar

1 teaspoon ground cumin

1 teaspoon liquid smoke

1 teaspoon onion powder

1 teaspoon smoked paprika

¾ cup vegetable broth

1 (32-ounce) can red kidney beans, drained

1 bunch scallions (white and green part), chopped

¼ cup chopped cilantro (optional)

In a medium pot, heat the olive oil. Add the chopped tomato, brown sugar, and ground cumin. Sauté until the tomato is soft, about 6 minutes or so. The juice from the tomato should be blended with the brown sugar and starting to appear thicker. Add the liquid smoke, onion powder, smoked paprika, and ¾ cup vegetable broth. Turn heat up until the sauce begins to bubble. After it has reached that point, turn the heat down to medium and add the beans. Cook on medium-low heat until the beans are tender and the liquid has cooked down and turned into a gravy that binds the dish.

Garnish with the scallions and chopped cilantro. Eat as is, with rice, or as the protein element in any of your favorite Latin recipes.

Irish Mushy Peas

Mushy peas are traditional United Kingdom pub fare. To make truly authentic mushy peas, you would use dried marrowfat peas, which despite their name are actually vegan. Marrowfat peas are merely matured green peas that dried out before harvest. They are larger than regular peas. If you can find these, they are a treat. Otherwise, regular frozen peas (preferably English) work well. The larger the pea the better, so avoid anything labeled "petite."

Serves 4

1 (10-ounce) package frozen green peas (not petite)

1 tablespoon vegetable oil

2 tablespoons tofu-based/vegan sour cream

2 tablespoons plain unsweetened dairy-free milk of your choice (avoid coconut)

½ teaspoon salt

pinch fresh ground black pepper

Place the frozen peas in a wide-bottomed pot and cover with water. Bring to a boil and cook for about 3 minutes or until the peas are tender enough to be mashed with a fork.

Drain the peas and put the vegetable oil in the now-empty pot. Heat the oil on medium-low heat, add the peas, vegan sour cream, milk, salt, and pepper and mash with a potato masher or the back of a slotted spoon, stirring constantly until most (but not all) of the peas are mashed and the peas are nice and hot. Serve.

Green Beans Amandine

Green beans amandine is a simple but delicious French side dish. Always an elegant and easy option, it pairs with many different types of cuisines (it's a wonderful way to "dress up" some classic BBQ fare). You want the almonds toasted until golden brown but not burned. Toasted nuts are culinary magic; burned nuts are terribly bitter. I always have a bag of green beans in the freezer for last-minute dinner ideas, but fresh will work even better. Avoid canned green beans. If you do use frozen, skip buying the "French cut" green beans. They are a little too thin and will get too wilted for this recipe.

Serves 6

1 pound fresh green beans, cut into 2-inch pieces, or 1 (16-ounce) bag of frozen cut green beans

½ cup whole, sliced, or slivered almonds

2 tablespoons olive oil

juice of half a lemon

kosher salt

fresh black pepper

Fill a large pot with salted water and bring it to a boil. After boiling, add the green beans, cover, and cook until the beans are cooked but not mushy, about 12 minutes. Drain and cover the beans so they stay warm.

While the beans are cooking, toast the almonds in a frying pan on medium-high heat, stirring occasionally until the almonds have picked up a nice golden color and are beginning to give off a wonderful aroma. If using whole almonds, cut them into pieces or blitz in a food processor until broken but not powdered.

Add the beans to the frying pan and drizzle with the olive oil, lemon juice, almonds, and salt and pepper to taste. Stir to combine and cook just until heated. Serve.

Green Bean Casserole

Oh, green bean casserole. I've been through every version of this imaginable; I have to say that the classic way that we've all probably had with the mushroom soup and fried onions from a can is a great base, but we can do better. Fried shallots are used in this recipe, but you can use regular onions if you prefer. Vidalia onions add a nice sweetness when fried, and raw dehydrated onion rings are also a tasty option.

Serves 8 to 10

2 tablespoons olive oil

1 onion, sliced thin

2 tablespoons all-purpose flour

1 shallot, diced

10 ounces white button mushrooms

½ cup vegan sour cream

2 teaspoons soy sauce

½ teaspoon apple cider vinegar

⅛ teaspoon cayenne

½ teaspoon salt

1 pound green beans, trimmed

In a large saucepan, heat the oil on medium-high heat. Dredge the sliced onion in the flour and fry it in the oil until crispy, about 8 to 10 minutes. Set the fried onion aside on a paper towel–lined plate.

Preheat the oven to 350°F.

In the same pan, with the remaining oil, sauté the shallot until softened, about 5 minutes. Add the mushrooms and stir. Take the pan off the heat and stir in the sour cream. Add ¾ cup water, the soy sauce, vinegar, cayenne, and salt while stirring constantly. Bring to a simmer and cook for 5 minutes.

Place the green beans into a large (9- by 13-inch or similar sized) casserole dish and pour the mushroom sauce over the green beans. Bake uncovered for 30 minutes. Top with the fried onions and serve.

Panelle
(Chickpea Fries)

Panelle, or chickpea fries, as a growing number of hip New York City restaurants are beginning to refer to them, started as a Sicilian street food. Classically one would find fried squares of this chickpea-based batter on top of a sandwich covered in ricotta and perhaps another cheese on a hard roll, which is just too much white and beige and too many starches for one meal in this author's opinion. Besides, that's far from vegan. Instead opt to make slightly healthier (or at least fancier) fries as a unique side dish to go with your "meat" balls. Chickpea flour can often be found in Indian or Middle Eastern groceries under the name gram flour. The recipe is deceptively simple.

Serves 4 to 6

This recipe requires resting the dough overnight.

2 cups chickpea flour (also known as gram flour)

1 teaspoon salt, plus more for topping

½ teaspoon smoked paprika

2⅓ cups water

oil for frying

Mix the chickpea flour, salt, and paprika in a medium-sized pot with the heat off. Slowly add the water while stirring constantly to get a nice smooth paste that is free of lumps.

On medium-high heat bring this batter up to a boil while whisking constantly. The mix will begin to get really thick and resemble polenta. Continue to whisk and boil for about 5 to 7 minutes. The batter should be smooth and as thick as porridge.

Lay out a few layers of plastic wrap onto a large cookie pan. Spread the chickpea batter onto the plastic as thinly as you want your finished product to be. Wrap the top of the *panelle* with more plastic wrap (making contact with the golden goodness) and move the tray to the fridge. Refrigerate overnight.

In a deep skillet or pan, heat up enough oil for frying. The oil is ready after a droplet of water creates splattering. Cut the panelle into strips for fries or larger shapes for sandwiches.

Fry the legume-based fries until golden brown. Rest on a paper towel to avoid too much grease and top with salt and any other spices you might desire. Best if enjoyed immediately.

Homage Hummus

I was slow to get on the hummus train, but once I did, I got on it with a vengeance. They say you never forget your first, and although this version is far from traditional, it *is* excellent. The recipe originally was inspired by a famous TV chef, but I like to add some peanuts and other spices to that chef's idea to get a little extra zing.

Serves 4

3 cloves garlic

pinch kosher salt

pinch black pepper

1 (15-ounce) can chickpeas (drain and keep half the liquid)

2 lemons, juiced

1 teaspoon paprika

2 tablespoons smooth peanut butter

⅓ cup extra-virgin olive oil

⅓ cup roasted salted peanuts

In a food processor, mince the garlic finely with the salt and black pepper.

Add the chickpeas, the saved liquid, the lemon juice, paprika, and peanut butter. Process until smooth. You do not want chunks of chickpeas. After everything is well blended and smooth, while the processor is running, drizzle in the olive oil.

Add the peanuts and process until they are chopped but still chunky. Enjoy.

Main Dishes

Feijoada (Brazilian Black Beans and Seitan)

Feijoada is a stew from Brazil that is typically very full of meat. Liquid smoke and seitan, however, add some depth of flavor and textures to this homage to Brazil's national dish.

Serves 4 to 6

2 tablespoons olive oil

2 cups onion, chopped

8 ounces spicy seitan

2 tablespoons chopped garlic

2 bay leaves

⅛ teaspoon cayenne pepper

1 teaspoon liquid smoke

¾ teaspoon salt

⅛ teaspoon freshly ground pepper

1 pound black beans

hot sauce

cooked rice

sautéed greens (collard, chard, or kale)

orange slices

In a large pot on medium-high heat, heat the olive oil. Sauté the onions and seitan until browned, about 7 minutes, making sure to stir occasionally. Add the garlic and sauté for another minute. Add bay leaves, cayenne, liquid smoke, 8 cups of water, salt, pepper, and black beans. Bring to a boil, reduce heat, cover, and simmer for approximately 2½ hours. If necessary, add more water during cooking to make sure the beans do not dry out. Using a spoon, mash half of the beans and stir. Taste for seasonings and add hot sauce to your liking. Serve with rice and greens, topped with orange slices.

Bean Burrito

Burritos. No one really knows who created them, but everyone loves them. In Mexico burritos are often a simple two-ingredient affair, a tortilla on the outside and either meat or refried beans on the inside. It's in the United States where the burrito gets its all-out treatment, being stuffed with all manner of foods from rice, to beans, to veggies. This is a great starting recipe to make your first or 50th burrito.

Makes 2 burritos

2 10-inch soft flour or corn tortillas

3 tablespoons vegetable oil

1 yellow onion, chopped

1 teaspoon minced jalapeño peppers

½ teaspoon salt

½ red bell pepper, chopped fine

1 clove garlic, minced

1 teaspoon ground cumin

1½ cups cooked black beans, either 1 (15-ounce) can or 1½ cups home-cooked

⅓ cup vegan sour cream

1 green onion, sliced thin

salsa (optional)

Using either a microwave or an oven, prepare the tortillas. If using a microwave, cover tortillas with a slightly dampened paper towel and microwave on half power for 2 minutes. Set aside. If using the oven, preheat to 350°F. Cover the tortillas in aluminum foil and bake for approximately 15 minutes or until nice and warm.

In a large pan, heat the vegetable oil on medium-high heat. Sauté the onion, jalapeño, salt, and bell pepper, stirring occasionally until the onion and pepper are softened, about 7 minutes. Add the garlic and cumin and stir for another minute. Add the beans and cook until everything is well heated.

Add the vegan sour cream and stir until everything is combined and hot. Add the green onion and mix.

Fill the warmed tortillas and roll up into that iconic burrito shape. Top with more sour cream, some salsa, and green onions if so desired.

Falafel

Falafel are very versatile. You can put them on a salad or eat them on their own or served with hummus. You can put them inside a pita with some tomato and onions or stuff them into a pressed sandwich. You can do whatever you want with them, but you can't go wrong.

Serves 4

¼ cup oil for frying

1 (15-ounce) can chickpeas, rinsed and drained

1 large onion, chopped

½ cup parsley leaf, chopped

½ cup baby spinach

2 cloves garlic, minced

2 green onions, chopped

2 teaspoons ground cumin

1 teaspoon ground coriander

1 teaspoon salt

⅛ teaspoon fresh black pepper

⅛ teaspoon cayenne pepper

1 teaspoon lemon juice

1½ tablespoons olive oil

1 teaspoon baking powder

1 cup dry breadcrumbs

In a medium saucepan, heat ¼ cup of oil on medium-high heat to fry your falafel.

In the bowl of a food processor, blend the chickpeas, onion, parsley, baby spinach, garlic, green onions, cumin, coriander, salt, black pepper, cayenne, and lemon juice. After this has blended thoroughly, drizzle in the olive oil while chopping until it is all well combined but not smooth.

Transfer the paste into a large mixing bowl and stir in the baking powder and half of the breadcrumbs. The falafel should keep together but not feel wet or too sticky. If the mix is too wet, add more of the breadcrumbs. After the dough is ready, wet your hands and shape it into balls about 1½ inches in diameter.

Fry the falafels in the hot oil, turning once so each side is well browned, about 3 minutes per side. After they are done, set them aside to rest on a paper towel until serving.

Italian "Meat" Balls

Meatballs seem to have gained in popularity over the last few years, which is hard to imagine as even possible because most households around the world have already been serving local variations of ground meat shaped into balls. The Italian seasonings are the ones with which Americans are most familiar, and the cannellini beans make the perfect meat replacement.

Serves 6 to 8

½ yellow onion, grated

2 cloves garlic, minced

¼ cup chopped parsley

1½ teaspoons dried oregano

½ cup dried breadcrumbs

½ teaspoon kosher salt

½ teaspoon freshly ground black pepper

1 roasted red bell pepper, seeded and chopped

2½ cups cooked cannellini beans

1 tablespoon freshly ground flax seed mixed into 3 tablespoons of water

marinara sauce of your choice

cooked pasta

Use either a nonstick baking sheet or a regular baking sheet that has been sprayed with a nonstick additive or well oiled. Preheat the oven to 350°F.

In a medium-sized bowl, combine the onion, garlic, parsley, oregano, breadcrumbs, salt, and pepper.

In a food processor, combine the bell pepper, beans, and flax seed mixed with water. Mix until well chopped and combined but not smooth. Mix this into the breadcrumb mixture.

Portion the mixture into balls about 2 tablespoons in size. Use your hands to compress and roll the mixture into ball shapes. Arrange the balls onto the baking sheet, making sure to leave space in between each ball, or else they will stick together. Bake for 10 minutes, rotate the pan 180 degrees, and bake for another 10 minutes or until the balls are firm and golden brown.

Heat up your pasta sauce in a large saucepan and add your cooked "meat" balls, stirring to ensure each ball is bathed in sauce. Simmer for another 10 minutes. Serve on your favorite pasta.

Green Bean Curry

Spices are the easiest way to get the most bang for your caloric buck, and nearly everyone loves a good curry. This is one of those dishes that's perfect if you're watching your wallet and/or your waistline but you refuse to compromise on taste.

Serves 4 to 6

1 teaspoon salt, plus more if needed

1 pound green beans, trimmed and cut into 1-inch pieces

4 red wax potatoes, cubed

8 ounces baby spinach, chopped

2 tablespoons olive oil

1 large yellow onion, sliced

1-inch piece ginger, minced

1 tablespoon garam masala

1½ teaspoons turmeric

1½ teaspoons ground coriander

1½ teaspoons ground cumin

1½ teaspoons brown mustard seeds

½ teaspoon smoked paprika

½ teaspoon cayenne

3 cloves garlic, minced

In a large saucepan, bring 3 cups of salted water to a boil on high heat. You want the water to be as salty as ocean water. Add the green beans and potatoes, cover, and then reduce to a simmer. Simmer for 15 minutes. The potatoes should still be firm, but the green beans should be nice and soft. Add the chopped spinach. Cook for 3 minutes and then set the heat to the lowest setting.

In a large sauté pan, heat the olive oil on medium-high heat and sauté the onion until it begins to get soft but not browned, about 5 minutes, being sure to stir from time to time. Add the ginger and cook for another 2 minutes. Add the spices and cook for another couple minutes. Your kitchen should smell amazing at this point. Add the garlic and cook for one minute.

Move all the potatoes, beans, and spinach into the large pan with the spiced onions and stir together. Cook while stirring for another 5 minutes or until heated throughout and all the ingredients are well combined. Add salt to taste.

Black Bean and Sweet Potato Queso-Less-Dillas

The recipe is a personal interpretation of just a handful of the delightful flavors of Mexico. The creamy richness of the sweet potato perfectly takes the place of the cheese, or queso, as they say in Mexico, for a flavorful queso-less-dilla. The spice of the jalapeño and the distinctly tropical tart of the lime tie this dish together. Feel free to add other veggies such as sautéed zucchini, greens, or whatever you like.

Serves 3 to 4

1 bay leaf

1 jalapeño, seeded and halved

1 teaspoon salt, plus more for seasoning

1 medium sweet potato, peeled and cut into cubes

¼ cup vegetable oil

1 medium onion, chopped

½ green bell pepper

2 cloves garlic, minced

1 cup cooked black beans

juice from 1 lime

tortillas as needed, at least 2 per queso-less-dilla

Bring a medium pot full of water to a boil. Add the bay leaf, half of the jalapeño, salt, and sweet potato. Cover and cook on medium heat until the sweet potato is tender but not mushy, about 15 minutes. Drain the sweet potato and discard the jalapeño.

Mince the remaining half of the jalapeño and reserve ½ teaspoon (or more if you like it spicy).

While the sweet potato is halfway through cooking, heat the vegetable oil in a large pan on medium-high heat. Sauté the onion and bell pepper until tender and translucent, about 7 minutes. Add the garlic and cook another half a minute.

Add the jalapeño, black beans, and sweet potato to the frying pan and cook, using a spatula to stir while partially mashing the sweet potato until the mixture holds together but is not completely smooth. Squeeze the lime juice over the potatoes. Set aside this mixture; it will be your filling. Wipe the frying pan clean.

In the frying pan, place one tortilla and cover it with the filling, spread out evenly. Top with another tortilla and cook on medium-high heat for about 6 minutes; flip and cook until the tortillas are slightly crisped and the filling is heated. Continue with the rest of the tortillas and filling, or save the filling to eat topped on rice.

Black Bean Burgers

Perfect for grilling days or days when you need to be reminded of summertime cookouts, or just any old time you want a burger.

Serves 4

½ green bell pepper, chopped

½ onion, chopped

1 tablespoon vegetable oil

3 cloves garlic, peeled

1 pound black beans, soaked overnight, then drained and rinsed

2 teaspoons ground cumin

1 tablespoon seasoned salt

1 teaspoon sriracha

¾ cup breadcrumbs

In a medium-sized pan on medium-high heat, sauté the bell pepper and onion, stirring occasionally in the oil until softened, about 7 minutes. Add the garlic and cook another minute. Set aside and allow to cool.

In the bowl of a food processor, chop the black beans into a thick paste. Add the onion, bell pepper, garlic, cumin, seasoned salt, and sriracha and pulse until the onions and peppers are small pieces and the spices have been blended in. Transfer this mixture to a bowl.

Add the breadcrumbs and stir the mixture with a spatula or wooden spoon. Shape this batter into patties approximately ½ inch thick, freeze, and bake frozen at 375°F for 10 minutes on each side or fry on medium-high heat in vegetable oil for approximately 8 minutes each side.

Curried Dal with Cauliflower

The colors of this dish are lovely. The turmeric dyes the cauliflower, and the green spinach stands out against the otherwise sea of yellow. This recipe also works very well with potatoes in the place of cauliflower.

Serves 4

1 cup dried yellow split peas

1 bay leaf

2 cups chopped cauliflower

1½ teaspoons salt

1½ tablespoons coconut oil

½ onion, chopped

1½ teaspoons fresh ginger, peeled and minced

2 cloves garlic, minced

1 tablespoon cumin seeds

1 tablespoon brown mustard seeds

1½ teaspoons ground coriander

1 teaspoon ground turmeric

½ teaspoon ground red pepper

4 cups spinach, torn

In a large pot, bring 2½ cups water to a boil. Add the split peas and bay leaf. Cover partially, reduce heat, and simmer for 45 to 50 minutes or until the peas are nice and tender but not mushy. Add the cauliflower, salt, and 1 cup water. Bring to a boil once more. Uncover, lower the heat, and simmer until the cauliflower is very tender, about 20 minutes. Stir from time to time to make sure the peas do not stick to the bottom. Turn off the heat and remove the bay leaf.

In a small pan, heat the coconut oil on medium-high heat. Sauté the onion and ginger for 5 minutes. Add the garlic, cumin, mustard seeds, coriander, turmeric, and red pepper. Lower the heat to low and cook for 2 minutes while stirring. Add this spice mix to the large pot and simmer for 15 minutes uncovered. The peas should be nice and thick. Add the spinach and cook until it softens, about 3 minutes.

Chana Masala

Chana masala is one of India's most well-known curry dishes. It's a great introduction to the classic flavors of curry, turmeric, cumin, coriander, ginger, and more. Curry is a totally personal experience, with some people desiring more cumin or less, and so on. After you get comfortable with these spices, a wonderful world of flavors awaits you.

Serves 6

2 tablespoons vegetable oil

2 yellow onions, diced

1 tablespoon ginger, grated

4 garlic cloves, minced

2 hot green chiles, stemmed and cored, chopped fine

1 teaspoon cumin seeds

2 teaspoons garam masala

2 teaspoons ground coriander

2 teaspoons ground cumin

½ teaspoon cayenne

1 teaspoon kosher salt

½ teaspoon turmeric

1 (28-ounce) can chopped peeled tomatoes, with juice

2 (15-ounce) cans chickpeas, drained and rinsed, or 4 cups cooked chickpeas

juice of one lemon

In a large stock pot, heat up the oil on medium-high heat. Cook the onions, ginger, garlic, and chiles until softened and browned, about 7 minutes.

Add the spices and cook while stirring constantly for about three minutes. Add the tomatoes and their juices. Mix well. Add 1 cup of water and the chickpeas. Simmer for 15 minutes. Add the lemon juice and stir to combine.

Chickpea Couscous

Couscous can be prepared either steamed on the stovetop, which is the more traditional way, or in the microwave, which is the faster and easier way. In order to microwave your couscous, mix 1 part couscous to 2 parts water and cover it. Microwave this on high for 2 to 3 minutes and then allow to rest for 3 minutes before uncovering and fluffing with a fork and checking for doneness. Mint really brightens a dish like this, and it is a staple of Middle Eastern cooking.

Serves 4

½ red onion, diced

3 tablespoons olive oil

2 lemons, juiced and zested

1 clove garlic, minced

1 (10-ounce) box couscous, steamed or microwaved and cooled

½ cup raisins

1 (15-ounce) can chickpeas, drained and rinsed

1 cup red bell pepper, chopped and seeded

2 cups cucumbers, chopped

½ cup fresh parsley, chopped

½ cup fresh mint, chopped

salt and pepper

In a very large bowl, mix together your onion, olive oil, lemon juice, lemon zest, and garlic. Stir until well combined.

Add the remaining ingredients and toss to coat. Add more lemon if you so desire (salt and pepper to taste) and serve.

Ful Medames (Egyptian Favas)

Ful medames, or Egyptian-style favas, are a staple meal in the Middle East. This is Egypt's national dish, and it is very common to find these stewed favas served in homes or for sale by street vendors as a common breakfast. As with almost any recipe in this book, this dish is meant to be played around with a bit to find the level of spice that is most to your liking. This recipe works well with the addition of ground cumin, cayenne, sumac, or aleppo pepper flakes. Traditionally this dish is served with flatbreads, pickled vegetables, and fresh arugula. For the Greek Island version, try topping the favas with picked red onions and serve it as a side dish with some pita bread.

Serves 2 to 4

2 cups favas, soaked overnight
1 small onion, chopped fine
4 cloves garlic
¼ cup olive oil
2 lemons
⅓ cup chopped parsley
salt and black pepper

Drain and rinse the soaked favas. Put the beans and onion into a medium pot and cover with water by at least 1 inch. Bring to a boil and boil for 2 minutes. Then reduce the heat and simmer gently for about 2 hours, or until the beans are nice and tender.

Mash the garlic with the back of a fork and enough salt to create a paste. Set aside.

After the beans are tender, turn the heat back up and cook the liquid down until you are basically creating a thick stew of beans. Add black pepper to taste, olive oil, and garlic and begin to mix roughly with a spatula, pressing and breaking some of the beans in the process.

After the beans are mostly mashed and the oil, garlic, and pepper are mixed in take this off of the heat and transfer to a serving plate.

Drizzle with a little more olive oil if desired and the juice of one lemon. Quarter the other lemon and serve alongside the favas. Sprinkle with the parsley before serving.

Jamaican Peanut Porridge

Peanuts are common in a lot of African cuisine, and they made their way over to the Caribbean due to this. For an American unfamiliar with this type of dish, it's a wonder to stumble across. If you like peanut butter, you'll like this porridge. It's basically peanut butter–flavored oatmeal served hot for breakfast. It's high in protein and a yummy way to start your day the Jamaican way. You will need peanuts for this; peanut butter just doesn't work the same.

Serves 1 to 2

1 cup oatmeal (quick cooking is fine; instant is not)
1 cup shelled raw peanuts
½ teaspoon salt
1 tablespoon flour
⅛ teaspoon fresh grated mace or nutmeg
1 tablespoon cornmeal
½ teaspoon vanilla extract
¾ cup coconut milk
water as needed

In a food processor, grind the oatmeal into a powder. Set aside. In the same food processor, grind the peanuts until they are almost a smooth peanut butter.

In a small pot, bring 1 cup of water to a boil with the salt.

While the water is coming to a boil, mix together the flour, powdered oatmeal, peanuts, mace or nutmeg, and cornmeal into a medium-sized bowl.

Using a spatula, stir in water (not the boiling water) until a loose, liquid paste is formed, which will take about 1 cup of water or so. This paste should be wet enough to be able to be poured.

Pour this paste into the boiling water. Stir until no lumps remain.

Reduce heat and cover partially, cooking on medium heat for about 15 minutes, stirring occasionally to prevent the bottom from sticking to the pot and burning.

Remove the lid and add the vanilla and the coconut milk. Cook on medium-high heat until the porridge no longer has a taste of raw flour and is the consistency you prefer, at least another couple of minutes. Serve.

Kinda Cassoulet

Cassoulet is exactly the kind of thing that you would never expect to find veganized. Originally a specialty of southern France (and the pride of the medieval city Carcassonne), it is most often eaten in cold weather. Traditionally it is full of duck, be it duck fat, duck skin, and/or duck sausage. However, it is *also* full of cannellini beans and a wonderful warming tomato sauce. The dish is a hearty casserole that has proved well worth the effort required to remove all the animal by-products. What is left is more true to the American cassoulet, which is now a catch-all term for any thick bean-based casserole. The smells that will fill your kitchen as the leeks and tomatoes bubble away are reason enough to try this.

Serves 4 to 6

3 leeks, dark green parts discarded

¼ cup olive oil

3 large carrots, cut in half lengthwise and then cut into chunks

3 celery stalks, cut into chunks

4 garlic cloves, diced

4 sprigs thyme

1 bay leaf

½ teaspoon kosher salt

½ teaspoon pepper

1 cup dried brown mushrooms, quartered, rehydrated, and 1 cup soaking water reserved

1 (19-ounce) can diced tomatoes, with juice

¼ cup tomato paste

4 cups cooked cannellini beans, or any white bean

2 links of vegan sausage, preferably andouille style

3 cups vegetable stock

4 cups plain breadcrumbs

2 tablespoons garlic salt

2 sprigs parsley, chopped

Cut the leeks in half lengthwise and then cut those halves in half lengthwise once more. Make sure to rinse very well. Allow to dry.

In a large pot, heat the olive oil on medium high and cook the leeks, carrots, celery, garlic, thyme, bay leaf, salt, and pepper. Make sure to stir every now and then to prevent the food from sticking to the pan. Cook until the leeks are soft and browned on their edges, or about 10 to 15 minutes. Add the mushrooms and 1 cup of their soaking water, tomatoes and their juice, tomato paste, cooked beans, vegan sausage, and vegetable stock. Lower the heat and allow to simmer half covered for about half an hour.

While the cassoulet cooks, toast the breadcrumbs with the garlic salt in a large fry pan, stirring so that they brown but do not burn.

Discard the thyme and bay leaf. Top the cassoulet with the breadcrumbs and parsley and serve.

Lentil Loaf

It's difficult to remember sometimes that culinary icons from the Americas that aren't regionally specific are still novel and unique to people living outside of the States and Canada. Paired with some greens and mashed potatoes, it's easy to see why this is such a classic.

Serves 4 to 6

1 cup green lentils

½ teaspoon salt, more if needed

3 tablespoons vegetable oil

1 onion, diced

1 stalk celery, diced

1 green bell pepper, diced

3 cloves garlic, minced

1 cup walnuts, toasted and ground

3 tablespoons ground flax, mixed with ½ cup warm water

¼ cup oatmeal, uncooked

2 slices stale bread, crumbled

¾ teaspoon dried thyme

3 tablespoons ketchup

¼ cup brown sugar

½ teaspoon dry mustard

½ teaspoon nutmeg

black pepper

Preheat the oven to 350°F.

In a medium pot bring 3 cups of water to a boil on medium high with the lentils and ½ teaspoon salt. Lower the heat to medium low and simmer the lentils for 45 minutes. Make sure to stir and watch this pot; you do not want to run out of water and may add more water as necessary. You want these lentils to be mushy.

In a large pan on medium-high, heat up 2 tablespoons of the vegetable oil. Sauté the onion, celery, and bell pepper, stirring occasionally for approximately 4 minutes. Add the garlic and cook for another minute while stirring.

In a large bowl, mix together the remaining ingredients. Add in the sautéed vegetables and lentils. Season with salt and pepper to personal preference.

Line a greased loaf pan with parchment paper. Very firmly press the loaf mix into the pan. Smooth out the top if need be. Cover with tinfoil. Bake on the middle rack for 30 minutes. Uncover and bake for another 15 minutes. Allow to cool for at least 15 minutes before slicing and serving.

Lentil Patties

Nothing says American summertime like a cookout. And nothing says cookout like a burger.

Serves 4 to 6

½ teaspoon salt

1 cup brown lentils

1 tablespoon olive oil

1 carrot, shredded

1 (1-ounce) packet onion soup mix

1 teaspoon red pepper flakes

1 tablespoon soy sauce

¾ cup rolled oats, ground fine

¾ cup breadcrumbs

¼ cup walnuts, toasted and ground

In a medium pot, boil 3 cups of water with salt. Add the lentils and boil uncovered for about 45 minutes or until the lentils are soft and the water is almost completely cooked off.

In a medium pan, heat the olive oil and sauté the shredded carrot for about 4 minutes or until the carrot is soft. Stir in the onion soup mix, pepper flakes, and soy sauce.

In a large bowl, mix the ground oats, breadcrumbs, and walnuts. Add the carrots and lentils. Mix everything until it holds together. Form the patties while the mixture is still warm.

Bake at 325°F for 15 minutes, pan fry or grill as you would any other patty.

Rice and Peas

Rice and peas is a misleading name. This staple dish from the Caribbean is actually rice with beans. Although you'll find it all throughout the region, this version hails from my time spent in Jamaica. The scotch bonnet pepper is optional, but I always include it. The heat created by it creates a nice depth of flavor and somehow makes even the hot Jamaican air feel cooler. The hotter the day, the spicier your meal should be.

Serves 4 to 6 as a side

½ pound (1 cup) dried kidney beans or small red beans, not soaked
6 to 8 cups coconut milk
1 teaspoon freshly ground black pepper
2 sprigs fresh thyme or 1½ teaspoons dried
2 whole scallions, crushed
scotch bonnet pepper (optional)
2 cups uncooked long-grain white rice
2 teaspoons salt

Sift the beans to remove any bad beans or small stones. Rinse the beans thoroughly under cold water and place them with the coconut milk in a medium-sized saucepan. Turn heat to high and bring to a boil. Reduce heat to low and add the black pepper, thyme, scallions, and scotch bonnet pepper (optional). Simmer this mixture covered for 1½ to 2 hours or until the beans are firm but close to being done. Add water as needed if the coconut milk cooks down and no longer covers the beans.

Add the rice, salt, and more water until the coconut milk/water mixture is 1 inch above the rice. Bring this back to a boil using high heat. Take the heat down to medium low and simmer the pot covered for 20 minutes. Remove the stems of the thyme (if using fresh), scallions, and scotch bonnet pepper. Toss gently with a fork and serve immediately.

New Year's Black-Eyed Peas

Deep in the south there is a tradition of eating black-eyed peas for good luck on New Year's Day. Black-eyed peas have a strong history of being "poor" food, and as the old saying goes, "Eat poor on New Year's Day, and eat fat all year." Just because these beans are considered poor food doesn't mean that they aren't rich in flavor.

Serves 6 to 8

2 tablespoons olive oil

1 large onion, chopped

2 stalks celery, chopped

2 cloves garlic, minced

2 tablespoons tomato paste

½ teaspoon crushed red pepper flakes

1 cup vegetable broth

3 cups water

1 bay leaf

½ teaspoon liquid smoke

2 cups dried black-eyed peas, soaked overnight

4 cups water

2 cups rice

salt and pepper

In a medium saucepan, heat the oil over medium-high heat. Cook the onion and celery, stirring occasionally until softened and browned, about 7 minutes. Add the garlic and cook while stirring another minute.

Add the tomato paste and pepper flakes and stir to combine well. Add the vegetable broth, 3 cups of water, bay leaf, liquid smoke, and soaked black-eyed peas. Bring to a boil, cover, and reduce the heat and simmer for about 45 minutes. The sauce should thicken but not be dry. If it is sticking to the bottom or getting too dry, add more water and stir well. After the black-eyed peas are tender and the sauce around them is thickened, the mixture is ready for the rice.

After the beans have been simmering for 15 minutes, in another saucepan bring 4 cups of water to a boil and add the two cups of rice. Cover, reduce the heat to medium low, and simmer the rice for approximately 20 minutes, or until the water has cooked off and the rice is tender. Let the rice rest for 10 minutes after cooking and then stir into the cooked black-eyed peas. Add salt and pepper to taste. Serve.

Samosas

Samosas take a little bit of effort, but they are well worth it. Make sure to work quickly with phyllo and only thaw what you need, because it doesn't refreeze well.

Makes 12 samosas

1½ tablespoons vegetable oil

½ cup carrot, chopped fine

½ cup green onion, sliced thin

2 tablespoons fresh ginger root, peeled and minced

1 tablespoon garlic clove, minced

1 tablespoon tomato paste

1½ teaspoons cumin seeds

1 teaspoon brown mustard seeds

¾ teaspoon kosher salt

¼ teaspoon ground red pepper

¼ teaspoon ground black pepper

1 cup thawed frozen green peas

1 (15-ounce) can chickpeas, rinsed and drained

1 tablespoon fresh lemon juice

½ cup fresh cilantro

24 sheets frozen phyllo dough, thawed

¼ cup olive oil

Preheat the oven to 400°F.

In a large skillet on medium heat, heat up the oil. Add the carrot, green onion, and ginger. Cook for about 5 minutes or until everything is softened, stirring often. Add the garlic and cook another minute, stirring the whole time. Now add the tomato paste, cumin, mustard seeds, salt, red pepper, and black pepper. Cook for another 3 minutes while stirring. Add the green peas, 1 tablespoon of water, and the chickpeas. Cook for 3 more minutes. Take off the heat and add the lemon juice and cilantro.

Take out one thawed sheet of phyllo and lay it out flat on a large work surface. Keep the rest of the phyllo covered with a damp cloth or paper towel (damp, not wet) so that they do not dry out. You have to work quickly with phyllo, or it dries out. Rub it lightly with a little olive oil. Place another sheet of phyllo on top of the oiled one. Fold these in half lengthwise.

Put about 2 tablespoons of the chickpea mixture onto the bottom of the sheets, being careful to leave a border of an inch. Fold the bottom corner over this mix, making a triangle. Continue to fold this up the phyllo, in a back and forth kind of motion, maintaining the triangle shape. Tuck any loose edges under and place the seam side on the bottom and rub the top with olive oil.

Continue with the rest of the phyllo and filling. Bake for 10 minutes or until golden brown and nice and crunchy.

Green Bean Stir Fry

This is an excellent healthy side dish for your next Asian-inspired meal. The crunchy green beans carry the nutty toasty flavor of the sesame oil and the tang of the vinegar well. It's a versatile recipe that goes with Japanese, Korean, Chinese, and even some Thai dishes. Feel free to add chile flakes, bell peppers, sprouts, mushrooms, or whatever you like.

Serves 6

2 tablespoons rice vinegar

1 tablespoon sesame oil

1 tablespoon ginger, peeled and grated

½ teaspoon salt

¼ teaspoon freshly ground black pepper

2 tablespoons vegetable oil

1 pound fresh green beans, washed and trimmed

1 small onion, diced

2 cloves garlic, minced

Mix the vinegar, sesame oil, ginger, salt, and pepper together. Set aside.

In a large skillet or wok, heat up the vegetable oil on medium-high heat. Add the green beans and onion, stirring often, and cook for approximately 4 minutes, or until the beans begin to soften. Add the garlic and continue to cook for another minute. Add the sauce and cook, stirring often until the beans are tender.

Southwestern Chili

This American-styled chili has the distinct flavor profile that comes from the Southwest region and its close proximity to Mexico.

Serves 6 to 8

2 tablespoons olive oil

1 yellow onion, chopped

1 green pepper, seeded and chopped

1 red pepper, seeded and chopped

1 poblano pepper, seeded and chopped

1 small jalapeño, seeded and chopped

4 cloves garlic, crushed and minced

1 cup pale beer or vegetable stock

1 cup cooked black beans

2 cups cooked dark red kidney beans

2 cans diced tomatoes, with juices

1 teaspoon ground cumin

½ teaspoon dried oregano

2 tablespoons cilantro

2 tablespoons chili powder

1 tablespoon hot sauce

2 teaspoons kosher salt

1 cup spicy vegetarian Mexican Refried Beans (page 48)

green onions, sliced

Cashew Sour Cream (page 43) or Tofu Sour Cream (page 44)

In a large pot on medium-high heat, heat up the oil. Sauté the onion, and all the peppers for about 7 minutes, stirring occasionally. Add the garlic and cook for another minute. Add the beer, black beans, kidney beans, tomatoes, cumin, oregano, cilantro, chili powder, hot sauce, and salt. Stir well to combine. Simmer for about 15 minutes, covered. Add the refried beans to thicken the chili. Simmer for another 5 minutes uncovered. Serve with green onions and sour cream.

South Indian *Dal Tadka*

New Jersey has a strong Indian populace, so much so that it is not unusual to find advertisements on local public transit in Hindi as well as English. It was in Jersey City that your author first discovered this dish, *dal tadka*. Very typical of southern Indian cuisine, with its use of mustard seeds and curry leaves, this dal (lentils are referred to in India) is rich and creamy without being heavy. The bright yellow color and earthy savory aroma make a bowl of this more inviting still. The asafetida powder can be considered optional, but please don't skip out on the curry leaves; you'll be glad you didn't. A lot of these spices create a sauce similar to a sambar-styled gravy. Curry leaves and mustard seeds are very common in southern Indian cooking.

Serves 2 to 4

2 tablespoons vegetable oil

pinch cumin seeds

tiny pinch asafetida/hing powder (optional)

pinch brown mustard seeds

half a medium onion, diced

2 cloves garlic, minced

¼ tablespoon chili powder

1 tablespoon garam masala

½ tablespoon ground coriander

4 curry leaves

4 to 5 long red whole chiles

1 cup yellow lentils

Put 2 tablespoons of oil into a large pan. Heat the oil up on medium-high heat. Add the cumin, asafetida/hing powder, and mustard seeds after a few seconds, when the oil is heated but not burning. Wait for the spices to crackle. Add your onions and garlic.

Add your chili powder, garam masala, ground coriander, curry leaves, and whole red chiles. Let the spices and curry leaves cook for about 2 minutes and take off the heat. Add the spice mix to a large pot.

Add the lentils and 3 cups of water. Bring to a boil. Reduce heat and simmer for 20 minutes, covered. Remove the cover and simmer for another 5 minutes before serving. This curry should be slightly wet, so add more water if you need.

Drinks and Desserts

Sweet Red Bean Paste

Anko, or sweet red bean paste, is extremely common in many Asian pastries. The concept might seem strange to our Western tastes, but just as we take peanuts (also a legume) and grind them up and cover the paste in chocolate, people in China, Korea, Japan, Thailand, and many other countries take the adzuki, or red bean, and soak them, blend them with sugar, and fry them until thickened into a delicious paste that finds itself in many of our other recipes. Don't knock it until you try it. This recipe makes about 1¾ cups of *anko*. You can easily double this recipe.

Makes 1¾ cups

⅔ cup adzuki beans, soaked overnight
½ cup white sugar
¼ cup vegetable oil

Rinse and drain the beans. Put the beans in a medium-sized pot and cover with water by about 1 inch and bring to a boil. Boil for 2 minutes. Reduce the heat and cook the adzuki on a simmer for about 1½ to 2 hours or until the beans are very soft. Drain the beans.

Without waiting for the beans to cool, place them in a blender or food processor with the ½ cup of sugar and blend/process into a smooth paste.

While the beans are blending, heat the vegetable oil in a large frying pan on medium-high heat. After the oil is giving off steam, add the bean paste and lower the heat to medium low. Use a spatula to spread and press the beans around in the oil and cook in this manner for about 3 to 4 minutes or until the beans are dry in appearance but holding together. Remove the beans from the heat and allow to cool before storing in your refrigerator. The paste will keep for about one week well refrigerated or 3 months in the freezer.

Black Bean Brownies

Either you've heard of this recipe before and love it or you are scratching your head and thinking, "There is no way this is going to be good." Trust me. It's good. It's really, *really* good. Also, this recipe benefits from the surprising bonus of being a gluten-free dessert option. So go ahead and try it. With about 5 to 10 minutes of actual active cooking time and a brief and inexpensive ingredient list (for which you probably already have everything already), you have nothing to lose and a delicious, fudgy, surprisingly guilt-free world to gain. Canned black beans are used in this recipe for convenience, and the point is to not taste that is made from beans so the quality of flavor is not as important, but feel free to substitute 2 cups of well-cooked black beans.

(Note: This recipe produces a more fudgelike brownie. If you prefer yours more on the cakelike side, double the amount of flax seeds and water.)

Serves 9 to 12

1 (15.5-ounce) can of black beans, rinsed and drained (or 2 cups of well-cooked black beans)

3 tablespoons vegetable oil (coconut oil can be used but will result in a slight coconut taste)

2½ tablespoons of fresh ground flax seeds whisked into 3 tablespoon of warm water

¼ cup sugar

¼ cup brown sugar

¼ cup and 1 tablespoon cocoa powder (sifted if need be)

1 teaspoon baking powder

pinch salt

1 teaspoon vanilla extract

1 teaspoon coffee (optional but worth it; can be left over from the morning)

1 teaspoon cinnamon

walnuts or dairy-free chocolate or carob chips for topping (optional)

Preheat the oven to 350°F.

Using either a food processor or blender, combine all ingredients except for toppings. Blend well, stopping at least once to scrape down the sides of the blender carafe and blending again. You do not want any large chunks of beans in this batter. It should be very smooth.

Pour batter into 8- by 8-inch glass baking dish.

Bake on middle rack of oven for 20 to 25 minutes, or until a knife poked into the center comes out clean.

Cool for at least half an hour before cutting and serving. (If you can stand the wait. This author had to eat a couple of hot and melty corners. She won't tell anyone if you do the same thing.)

Edamame Soy Milk

This is one way to get kids to drink soy milk; it's naturally green. For sheer convenience, this milk can't be beat. Take frozen edamame (which are already blanched), cook for 3 minutes, blend, strain, and drink. OK, there is a slight bit more to it than that, but basically that's it. Feel free to omit the salt and add spices such as vanilla or ginger to taste when blending. Using hot water when blending creates a smoother and milder milk, but you will have to wait longer to drink it. It's worth the wait.

Serves 2 to 3

3 cups boiling water (plus 2 additional cups water)
pinch of salt
1 cup shelled (and thawed if using frozen) edamame

Bring the 3 cups of water to a rolling boil. Add the pinch of salt.

Add the cup of shelled, thawed edamame and boil for 4 minutes.

Blend the boiling water (might need to let it cool slightly depending on your blender), edamame, and additional two cups of water.

Strain and refrigerate for up to a week, leaving it uncovered until fully cooled.

Enjoy.

Chickpea Cupcakes

These little darlings are chock full of fiber and protein, all while being vegan, gluten free, and versatile. Not to mention super easy.

Makes 12 regular sized cupcakes

2¾ cups chickpea flour (also known as gram flour)

½ teaspoon salt

¾ cup cocoa powder

1¾ cups sugar

1½ teaspoons baking powder

2 teaspoons baking soda

2 tablespoons freshly ground flax with ¼ cup water

2 teaspoons vanilla extract

½ cup vegetable oil

1 cup homemade soy milk (or your favorite dairy-free milk)

1 cup boiling water

Preheat the oven to 350°F.

In a large bowl, sift together the chickpea flour, salt, cocoa powder, sugar, baking powder, and baking soda.

In a small bowl, mix together your flax and water solution, vanilla, vegetable oil, soy milk, and boiling water.

Mix your liquids into your dry ingredients. Pour into your cupcake liners (filling only halfway).

Bake on the middle rack of your oven for approximately 25 minutes, turning halfway through the cooking. The top should be firm when done.

Top with your favorite frosting, some sweet bean paste, or some powdered sugar.

Japanese Red Bean Ice Cream

Sweetened red beans are a very common flavor for ice creams throughout Asia and are often the first time that Westerners experience this dessert legume. You will need an ice cream maker for this recipe.

Makes 1 quart, or 6 to 8 servings

2 cups coconut cream

1 cup almond milk

2 tablespoon tapioca syrup (can substitute brown rice flour, though it will affect the flavor)

⅔ cup sugar

pinch salt

½ cup almond milk

1½ tablespoons tapioca starch

1½ cups Sweet Red Bean Paste (page 109)

In a medium-sized saucepan, boil the coconut cream, almond milk, tapioca syrup, sugar, and pinch of salt. Remove from the heat.

In a small bowl, whisk together the ½ cup almond milk and the tapioca starch. Add the red bean paste and blend. Pour the mixture into to the saucepan and whisk vigorously. Bring to a simmer, stirring constantly for 5 minutes.

Strain and chill overnight.

Freeze using your ice cream maker's instructions. Allow to set in the freezer for a couple hours before serving.

Soy Milk

Homemade soy milk is easy. It just requires a little planning, and a nut milk bag helps too. Nut milk bags differ from cheesecloth in that the mesh is much finer. Cheesecloth will work in a pinch (make sure you line it in a colander or sieve first), but if you plan on making a lot of soy (or almond or other nut) milk, a nut milk bag is a worthwhile investment.

Serves 3 to 4

1 cup dried soybeans, soaked overnight and rinsed and drained

4 cups water

pinch of salt (kosher salt preferred)

2 tablespoons rolled oats

¼ teaspoon vanilla extract (optional)

1 teaspoon sugar (optional)

Rinse and drain soybeans a second time. Place the soybeans into the carafe of a powerful blender.

Bring 4 cups of water to a boil on high heat. Add this hot water, salt, and the oats to the carafe. Blend thoroughly.

Strain the mixture through a nut milk bag or cheesecloth-lined sieve into a large pot. Wring out as much liquid as you can. Cook the milk on medium-high heat until it begins to start simmering. Skim off the foam that forms at the top or any "skin" that occurs. Make sure to stir frequently. Cook for 20 minutes. Add the vanilla extract and any sugar.

Enjoy warm or allow to cool before refrigerating.

Korean Red Bean Soup

Soup might not strike you as an idea for dessert, but serve this chilled as is or warm and garnished with some chewy rice balls, and it's a welcome summertime treat. The balls need the soup to be warm or hot, or else they get unpleasantly hard.

Serves 4

RICE BALLS

½ cup hot water

pinch of salt

½ cup sweet rice flour (found in most Asian specialty groceries)

SOUP

1 cup adzuki beans

1 cup brown sugar

2 teaspoons salt

In a medium pot, bring 4 cups of water to boil on high heat. Add the adzuki beans to the boiling water and boil for 10 minutes. Reduce the heat, bringing it to a simmer, and cook for another hour. After the beans are tender, remove them from the heat and drain off the excess water.

While the beans cook, make the rice balls. Mix the hot water and salt into the sweet rice flour and mix with a spoon to combine. If the dough is too sticky to mix with your hands, add a little more rice flour and then knead the dough until well combined. After the dough is ready, pinch off small pieces and roll them into balls; set aside.

In a food processor or using a wooden spoon, mash the beans while adding in the brown sugar and salt. You want to mash or grind the beans into a thick paste.

Return the paste to the original pot and add ½ cup of sugar and 4 cups of water. Bring this to a boil, stirring well to break up the paste. Stir until the sugar is dissolved. After the sugar has dissolved, add the rice balls and cook for about 5 to 7 minutes, or until the rice balls have cooked all the way through.

Banana Soft Roll

Banana soft rolls with bean paste are a rather directly named sweet found in many bakeries throughout China and subsequently Chinatowns around the world. This is a fun and unique sweet that works great in packed lunches.

Makes approximately 16 bite-sized pieces

¾ cup sticky rice flour/glutinous rice flour

⅓ cup rice flour

3 tablespoons cooked sweet rice flour

½ cup sugar

½ teaspoon banana flavoring

6 to 8 tablespoons sweet red bean paste

Put about an inch of water into a large pot. Place either a steamer basket or flat-bottomed colander into the pot. Bring the water to a simmer.

Mix together all of your dry ingredients. Whisk in the banana flavoring and ⅔ cup of warm water (warm, not hot).

Spray a small pan that will hold your batter with nonstick cooking spray. Pour the batter into this pan (a pie pan works well). You might have to do this in two batches. Steam the batter for 25 minutes.

Remove from the steam and cover the top with 3 to 4 tablespoons of sweet red bean paste. Roll this up like a jelly roll and slice into bite-sized pieces. Serve.

Chinese Eight Treasure Rice

This recipe is vegan, but don't let that fool you into thinking that it's healthy by any stretch of the imagination. It is however beautiful, festive, and a rare treat. The festive nature of this dish is most apparent in its careful plating, which allows all of the fruits to show on the top of the dish. This dish is most often found on Chinese New Year or any other celebration feast.

Serves 8

2 cups uncooked sticky rice (might also be known as sweet rice), cooked

2 tablespoons sugar

4 tablespoons vegetable shortening

1 cup dried fruits of your choice (apricots, raisins, pineapple, figs, cranberries, and so on)

7 red maraschino cherries

1 cup Sweet Red Bean Paste (page 109)

SIMPLE SYRUP
½ cup water

½ cup sugar

1 tablespoon lemon juice

2 teaspoons cornstarch dissolved in 1 ½ tablespoons water

Prepare the sticky rice in a rice cooker or on the stove according to the directions on the package (but do not add any salt even if the recipe suggests it). Mix the cooked hot rice with ½ cup of hot water, the sugar, and the shortening.

While the rice is cooking, cut your dried fruits into decorative strips. Line the bottom of a medium bowl with the dried fruit pieces and the maraschino cherries, bearing in mind that however you place the fruit is how it will look after you invert the finished dish. The traditional pattern is to make the fruit take on the appearance of a blooming flower.

Place one-third of the cooked rice on top of the fruit. Press down firmly. Spread ½ cup of the sweet red bean paste over the rice and press it down so that it is all packed firm. Repeat this step with another third of the rice and the second half of the red bean paste. Finish by covering with the remaining rice and pack it all down very firmly!

Prepare the simple syrup by boiling all of the ingredients except for the cornstarch. After the sugar has completely dissolved, add the cornstarch that has been mixed with water. Cook until the liquid is once again clear and thick. Set aside.

To serve: invert the bowl onto a plate (place the plate upside down over the bowl and flip both at the same time). Drizzle the hot simple syrup over the rice and serve, using more syrup if you want.

Navy Bean Pie

The author discovered this unique pie only fairly recently. It goes by the name "Muslim bean pie" in many places. However, this is not an authentic Muslim recipe because some of the spices are not allowed within stricter sects of the religion.

Makes 1 pie

⅔ cup soy or rice milk powder mixed with ¾ cup water

¼ cup and 1 tablespoon ground flax seed mixed into ¼ cup and 2 tablespoons warm water

2 cups of cooked navy beans

½ cup sugar

¼ cup brown sugar

1 teaspoon cinnamon

1 teaspoon nutmeg

½ teaspoon kosher salt

½ teaspoon allspice

½ teaspoon ginger

1 9-inch pie shell, unbaked (either prebought vegan option or homemade)

While preparing the rest of the recipe, preheat the oven to 425°F.

In a blender or food processor, combine the soy or rice milk and water with the ground flax seeds and water until it becomes smooth and thick.

Add all of the remaining ingredients except the pie shell and blend until creamy and you no longer see chunks of beans. If needed, scrape the sides of the blender/food processor and blend again.

Pour mixture into unbaked pie shell and bake for 15 minutes.

Lower the temperature to 350°F and bake for another 35 minutes or until a toothpick poked into the center of the pie comes out clean. If there is cracking on the top of your pie, it is probably done. If the edges of the pie crust begin to get too dark, you can cover them with tin foil.

Pie can be served warm out of the oven or cold.

Chinese New Year Red Bean Pancakes

These light pancakes filled with sweetened red bean paste are exceptionally popular during the Chinese New Year. Folding the pancake in half when making them so that they are a half moon shape makes them resemble a coin purse, and consuming them is thought to welcome wealth and prosperity in the upcoming year.

Serves 4 to 6

boiling water

2 cups all-purpose flour

5 tablespoons vegetable oil

1 cup Sweet Red Bean Paste (page 109)

2 tablespoons white sesame seeds, toasted

Using either a stand mixer or a wooden spoon, mix ½ cup of the water into the flour. You might or might not need to add another ¼ cup of water. The dough should not be sticky. If mixing by hand, pour the dough out onto a work surface and knead until smooth, about 5 to 10 minutes. If using a stand mixer, mix on medium speed until smooth, about 5 minutes. Divide the dough in half and rest under a damp towel for a half hour.

Flour a large work surface. Roll out a half of the dough until ¼ inch thick. Using a cookie or biscuit cutter, cut out circles that are 3 inches in size. Rub the top of these circles with a little of the vegetable oil and stack them into groups of two with the oiled sides pressed together. Roll these stacked circles until doubled in size (about 6 inches). Cover these with a damp towel while you repeat these steps with the other half of the dough.

In a medium-sized frying pan on medium-high heat, cook each doubled up pancake, one at a time, until nice and brown; flip and cook until both sides are brown. Separate the pancakes and set them aside.

In the frying pan, heat up 2 tablespoons of oil. Place the pancakes' white (oiled) sides up and spread 2 teaspoons of the red bean paste on half of the pancake, making sure to not go over the edges. Fold the pancakes over in half and lightly pinch the edges together to hold the bean paste in. Fry these pancakes, cooking for 2 minutes on each side and flipping once. Garnish with the sesame seeds and serve, cutting the pancakes if so desired.

Common Conversions

1 gallon = 4 quarts = 8 pints = 16 cups =128 fluid ounces = 3.8 liters
1 quart = 2 pints = 4 cups = 32 ounces = .95 liter
1 pint = 2 cups = 16 ounces = 480 ml
1 cup = 8 ounces = 240 ml
¼ cup = 4 tablespoons = 12 teaspoons = 2 ounces = 60 ml
1 tablespoon = 3 teaspoons = ½ fluid ounce = 15 ml

Temperature Conversions

Fahrenheit (°F)	Celsius (°C)
200°F	95°C
225°F	110°C
250°F	120°C
275°F	135°C
300°F	150°C
325°F	165°C
350°F	175°C
375°F	190°C
400°F	200°C
425°F	220°C
450°F	230°C
475°F	245°C

Volume Conversions

U.S.	U.S. equivalent	Metric
1 tablespoon (3 teaspoons)	½ fluid ounce	15 milliliters
¼ cup	2 fluid ounces	60 milliliters
⅓ cup	3 fluid ounces	90 milliliters
½ cup	4 fluid ounces	120 milliliters
⅔ cup	5 fluid ounces	150 milliliters
¾ cup	6 fluid ounces	180 milliliters
1 cup	8 fluid ounces	240 milliliters
2 cups	16 fluid ounces	480 milliliters

Weight Conversions

U.S.	Metric
½ ounce	15 grams
1 ounce	30 grams
2 ounces	60 grams
¼ pound	115 grams
⅓ pound	150 grams
½ pound	225 grams
¾ pound	350 grams
1 pound	450 grams

Index

Cauliflower, 85; Dutch Split
Pea Soup, 24
String beans. *See* Green beans
Substitutions, 9
Sweet red bean paste
(ingredient): Banana Soft Roll,
117; Chinese Eight Treasure
Rice, 118–19; Chinese New
Year Red Bean Pancakes,
122–23; Japanese Red Bean Ice
Cream, 114
Sweet Red Bean Paste (recipe),
109

T
Temperature conversions, 124
Three-Bean Salad, 30
Tofu: Malaysian Vegetable Salad,
36–37; Miso Soup, 27; Tofu
Sour Cream, 44

Tofu sour cream (ingredient):
African Peanut Soup, 13; Irish
Mushy Peas, 65; Sour Green
Bean and Potato Soup, 16;
Southwestern Chili, 103
Tofu Sour Cream (recipe), 44
Tuscan White Bean Soup, 14–15

V
Valencian Minted Fava Salad, 31
Vegan sour cream: Bean Burrito,
74–75; Green Bean Casserole,
67. *See also* Cashew Sour
Cream; Tofu Sour Cream

W
White beans: Argentine White
Bean Salad, 32–33; *Gigandes*
(Greek Giant White Beans),
62–63; Kinda Cassoulet,
92–93; Tuscan White Bean
Soup, 14–15

Cauliflower, 85; Dutch Split
Pea Soup, 24
String beans. *See* Green beans
Substitutions, 9
Sweet red bean paste
(ingredient): Banana Soft Roll,
117; Chinese Eight Treasure
Rice, 118–19; Chinese New
Year Red Bean Pancakes,
122–23; Japanese Red Bean Ice
Cream, 114
Sweet Red Bean Paste (recipe),
109

T
Temperature conversions, 124
Three-Bean Salad, 30
Tofu: Malaysian Vegetable Salad,
36–37; Miso Soup, 27; Tofu
Sour Cream, 44

Tofu sour cream (ingredient):
African Peanut Soup, 13; Irish
Mushy Peas, 65; Sour Green
Bean and Potato Soup, 16;
Southwestern Chili, 103
Tofu Sour Cream (recipe), 44
Tuscan White Bean Soup, 14–15

V
Valencian Minted Fava Salad, 31
Vegan sour cream: Bean Burrito,
74–75; Green Bean Casserole,
67. *See also* Cashew Sour
Cream; Tofu Sour Cream

W
White beans: Argentine White
Bean Salad, 32–33; *Gigandes*
(Greek Giant White Beans),
62–63; Kinda Cassoulet,
92–93; Tuscan White Bean
Soup, 14–15

132

About the Author

Kelsey Kinser grew up in South Florida and dreamed of traveling to many distant lands. First, however, she went to Chicago, where she attended the renowned French Pastry School before moving to New York City, where she worked her way up to become a pastry chef in a popular group of restaurants. She took a year off from the city life to travel throughout Europe, where she worked in restaurants in France, Spain, and Greece. New York City, however, called her back and Kelsey currently resides and works in Brooklyn. When not cooking she enjoys exploring the city, playing board games, and going to comedy shows. This is her first book.